A HISTORY OF JEWISH COSTUME

BY THE SAME AUTHOR

Anglo-Jewish Portraits, 1935

A Jewish Iconography, 1954

FRONTISPIECE: MOROCCO 1832
MARIÉE JUIVE. *Water colour by E. Delacroix. Musée du Louvre*
She wears the traditional keswa el kbira *of a Jewish bride.*
Her wedding, which took place at Tangier, was attended by
Delacroix and became the subject of the painting in the Louvre.
Delacroix catalogue. *Arts Council 1964. Nos. 38 and 120.*

A HISTORY OF

JEWISH

COSTUME

by Alfred Rubens

Fellow of the Society of Antiquaries of London and
Fellow of the Royal Historical Society

FOREWORD BY JAMES LAVER

FUNK & WAGNALLS: NEW YORK

Published by FUNK & WAGNALLS
A Division of Reader's Digest Books, Inc., New York

© ALFRED RUBENS 1967

Library of Congress Catalog Card Number: 67-23303

Cover design by Abram Games
Book designed by L. René-Martin
Filmset, Printed and Bound in Great Britain by
Bookprint Limited, London and Crawley
Funk & Wagnalls, New York

Contents

Acknowledgements

I acknowledge gratefully the assistance I have received on many sides in connection with this book. Dr Richard Barnett initiated me into the mysteries of West Asian costume and placed at my disposal his unrivalled knowledge of the history and antiquities of that region. Mr Raphael Loewe provided invaluable help and advice in connection with the Hebrew and classical sources. Dr Cecil Roth has over the years supplied a vast amount of information and has been lavish with advice. Mr A. Schischa made a number of useful suggestions and translated some long passages from the Yiddish. It is also a pleasure to be able to express my appreciation to the Keepers, Librarians and staff at the British Museum, the Hebrew Union College, Cincinnati, the Hebrew University, Jerusalem, Jews' College, the London Library, the Mocatta Library, the Victoria and Albert Museum and the Warburg Institute for their unfailing courtesy and help.

A special word of thanks is due to Mr Abram Games for the cover design.

Among many others who have helped me I would like to thank the following: Mr J. Abecasis of Lisbon; Rev. E. S. Abinun; Mr C. Abramsky; Mr J. G. Ayers (Victoria and Albert Museum); Mr F. Caro of New York; Mr Sol Cohen (Hon. Curator, Jewish Museum, London); Mr Louis G. Cowan of New York; Mr D. Davidovitch (Museum of Ethnography and Folklore, Tel-Aviv); Mr H. Eisemann; Rabbi Dr Solomon B. Freehof of Pittsburg; Mrs L. Ginsburg (Victoria and Albert Museum); Mr Felix Gluck; Prof. E. R. Goodenough; Dr Joseph Gutmann (Hebrew Union College); Mrs P. Hart-Leverton; Dr H. Heimann (Warburg Institute); Mr J. C. Irwin (Victoria and Albert Museum); Dept. of Antiquities of The State of Israel; Mr D. King (Victoria and Albert Museum); Prof. Guido Kisch; Mrs A. Lancet-Müller (Bezalel National Museum, Jerusalem); Miss R. Lehmann (Jews' College Library); Mr Harold Levy; Prof. Bernard Lewis; Dr Jacob R. Marcus (Hebrew Union College); Mr J. Margolinsky (Jewish Museum, Copenhagen), Prof. B. Mark (Zydowski Instytut Historyczny,

Warsaw); Mr L. R. McColvin (Westminster City Librarian); Mr G. Meredith-Owens (British Museum); Mr Harvey Miller; Mr S. Noble (Yivo Institute, New York); Rev. Dr J. W. Parkes; Dr Arthur Polak of Amsterdam; Mr M. Prodan of Rome; Miss P. Quick; Dr J. Rosenwasser (British Museum); Mr. I. Shachar (Bezalel National Museum, Jerusalem); Mr Ernest Seligmann; The Swedish Institute (Mr P. A. Hildeman); Miss O. Tufnell; Mrs G. Weil.

Acknowledgements for kind permission to reproduce photographs are made to: Bayerisches Nationalmuseum; Bezalel Museum; Bibliothèque Nationale; Trustees of the British Museum; Copenhagen Museum; Hebrew Union College; Insurance Co. of North America; Jewish Museum, London; Jewish Theological Seminary; Mocatta Library; Musée du Louvre; Museum of Ethnography and Folklore, Tel-Aviv; National Trust; Public Record Office; Rijksmuseum; Spanish and Portuguese Synagogue; Royal Library, Copenhagen; Stadtarchiv, Coblenz; Stadtarchiv, Freiberg; Stadtarchiv, Worms; Stedelijk Museum, Amsterdam; University Library, Heidelberg; Victoria and Albert Museum; Yale University Library.

I wish to express my appreciation to the publishers and to the designer, Mrs Linda René-Martin, for their whole-hearted co-operation and for the enthusiasm with which they have handled the production of this book.

Finally a word of thanks to my Secretary, Mrs I. Karney, whose devotion and patience are matched only by her skill in deciphering my handwriting.

List of Illustrations

Unless otherwise stated the illustrations are taken from originals or photographs in the author's possession.

Rabbinical Dress
ASHKENAZI

Foreword

THE VAST MAJORITY of histories of costume are concerned with 'Fashion': that is, the changing styles worn by Western European women (for men hardly come into the picture) during the last six hundred years. It is only, after all, a very small part of the story.

'Fashion' is a function of the Renaissance, and it is no accident that Petrarch, 'the first modern man', should have entitled his most influential and popular work *The Triumph of Time*. For the greater part of human history, if you stayed where you were, your clothes never altered. But if you went into the next village, everything was different. This was to be subject to the tyranny of Place. But the whole meaning of the Renaissance, the whole meaning of modernity, the whole meaning of Fashion, is that we have substituted for the tyranny of Place the tyranny of Time. Go to the ends of the earth and everything is the same; but stay where you are in your little village for three months and all the women have different hats.

The Place-complex, if we may use the term, certainly fought a long rearguard action, in the sense that regional, that is to say national costumes were still recognizable as late as the seventeenth century. It was still possible to speak of French, English, Spanish, Italian and German costumes. But the immense prestige of Louis XIV brought it about that for the upper classes in Europe fashionable clothes henceforward meant French clothes. This dominance lasted, for both men and women, until the French Revolution, when the dictatorship of male attire passed to England. But Paris maintained its rule over women's clothes and, indeed, has kept it to this day.

Meanwhile, national and regional costume began to mean merely 'peasant' costume, which in some parts of Europe persisted until our own time. Up to a generation ago it was still possible when walking in the Tuileries Gardens to detect, from their costumes, which particular province of France the various nursemaids came from. Nowadays it would not be much of an exaggeration to say that in Western Europe at least, where regional costume persists it has been artificially preserved as a tourist attraction, although this is still not quite true of the Near East and the Balkans.

The final triumph of Time over Place means not only no distinction between the nations but no class distinction either, or so little that it would take an expert eye to detect it. There is not even a time-lag between the clothes of the upper and the lower classes. Everything is uniformly up-to-date.

That this represents a sad diminution in the variety and colour of life needs no stressing. Regional costume was often beautiful and redolent of the history of those who wore it. It is, in a sense, far more *interesting* than Fashion's vagaries, and it is, perhaps, surprising that the books which have been written about it are so few compared with the vast 'literature of Fashion'. Any new, authoritative book on the subject is worthy of welcome.

It is particularly welcome in the case of the Jewish people, for the problem of presentation is here immensely complex. The long period of time covered by its history and the fact that Jewish communities have been scattered all over the world and so have absorbed and reflected the costume of many different periods and places, add to the difficulty of presenting a coherent picture. And in addition to all this is the fact that Jews have frequently been *compelled* to adopt a special costume, often imposed as a mark of contempt but finally accepted as a badge of honour. The characteristic dress of the Polish Jew, for example, although not as common as it was fifty years ago, can be seen in certain parts of London even today.

Yet Jews, no more than Gentiles, have been able to escape the triumph of Time. All over the world they are losing their distinctive dress, and it was high time that a museum of Jewish costume should have been established in Israel. In another generation it might have been too late. It is therefore particularly appropriate at this time that Mr Alfred Rubens should have produced so learned and far-reaching a study as his *History of Jewish Costume*, and all those who are interested not only in Jewish costume as such but in costume in general are deeply in his debt.

JAMES LAVER

דבר אל בני ישראל ואמרת אלהם
ועשו להם ציצת על כנפי בגדיהם לדרתם
ונתנו על ציצת הכנף פתיל תכלת

Speak unto

the children of Israel

and bid them

to make a tassel on the corners

of their garments

throughout

their generations and to

put on it a

twined cord of blue

NUMBERS XV 38

במתא שמאי בלא מתא תותבאי

At home

you know the name, abroad

the costume

TALMUD B. SHABBAT 145B

Introduction

'THEN THE EYES of both of them were opened, and they perceived that they were naked; and they sewed together fig leaves and made themselves loincloths'.[1]

Adam and Eve became concerned about their nudity only after they had acquired Knowledge and indeed it is now generally accepted that modesty is a sophisticated feeling unknown to primitive man. Equally the modern view, that dress originates from the urge for decoration, is not in conflict with Jewish teaching. According to the rabbis 'the Lord's glory is man and man's ornament is his clothes';[2] clothes were more important than food and drink and one was enjoined to dress according to one's means but to eat and drink below one's means.[3]

As far as the evidence goes, the Jews in Biblical times dressed like their neighbours but there may have been some fine distinctions of shape or colour about their garments which are unknown to us. The tassels (Heb. *tsitsith*) prescribed in Numbers xv:38 and Deuteronomy xxii:12 are found on pagan dress, although perhaps without the blue (Heb. *techeleth*) dye, while the side locks (Heb. *peoth*) which are supposed to be derived from Leviticus xx:27 were also worn by several other peoples of the Ancient Near East.

Custom and *costume* are not only the same word, they are inseparable and their intimate connection manifests itself throughout the course of Jewish history by the tenacity with which both were guarded. The equivalent Hebrew word is *minhag* and it is not without significance that books of *Minhagim* with woodcuts showing the dress for the occasion began to appear soon after the introduction of engraving, despite the traditional Jewish aversion to figurative art. Zephaniah's attack on the princes who wore 'strange apparel' and the opposition

[1] Genesis iii : 7   [2] Midrash Tanhuma iii : 7b   [3] Mishnah. *Hullin* 84b

aroused by Jason's attempt to introduce a Greek hat[4] do not imply that Jewish costume was static; but changes occurred so slowly as to be almost unnoticeable and the resistance to change is its chief feature. This was not due merely to conservatism but because until comparatively modern times nothing was known about ancient costume and it was thought by Jews and Christians alike that the dress worn by old people went back to time immemorial. After a generation or two fashions formerly regarded as outrageous were accepted without question, but the rejection of anything new explains most of the peculiarities of Jewish costume.

The Jewish sumptuary laws were designed only partly to curb extravagance and ostentation; their object also was to prevent the adoption of new fashions, or what was known in Hebrew as *chukkath hagoyyim* and one finds next to a prohibition of some novelty a reminder of Leviticus xviii:3 which is the key to the Jewish attitude on this subject: 'you shall not copy the practices of the land of Egypt where you dwelt or of the land of Canaan to which I am taking you nor shall you follow their customs'. This is the basis for the more comprehensive prohibition found in the *Shulhhan Aruch*.[5]

The oldest survivals are found in the synagogue, just as examples of early Christian dress survive in the church. This to a certain extent must be due to the long-standing Jewish tradition of reserving special clothes for the Sabbath[6] which outlasted everyday clothes and in the course of time became established as synagogue wear until some major upheaval occurred. It may explain the survival of the *sargenes* or *kittel*, a garment for special ritual occasions inherited from Talmudic times and the *tallith* which is derived from the Roman

---

[4] See p. 13   [5] See p. 91

[6] The special Sabbath dress was considered so important that if it was worn on a weekday by mistake it became unclean (Talmud B. *Hagigah* 20a).

pallium. Even the last war has not completely eliminated the traditional silk hat for synagogue use in England.

In Roman times a married woman who had her head completely covered was assumed to be a Jewess[7] while a *pallium* with *tsitsith* attached to its corners distinguished Jews and Christians alike from pagans. The first evidence of a universal Jewish costume is the Jewish hat of medieval times which was probably derived from a tall cone-shaped hat formerly worn in Persia and retained by Jews when followers of the Prophet adopted the turban. For several centuries it was the badge and symbol of a Jew, worn voluntarily and with pride; the Jew and his hat were inseparable and the importance of the hat in Jewish ritual, which is a comparatively modern development, seems to date from this time.[8]

With their pointed hats and long beards the Jews could be easily identified and it was only when they began to drop these distinctions that the Church in the thirteenth century introduced the Badge or made the wearing of the hat compulsory.

Since that time until the last century there has been a recognized Jewish mode of dress in practically every country where Jews lived. In those countries like Holland, America and England where Jews dressed like Christians the fact that they did so is in itself significant and indicates the extent to which they had become integrated.

There is no traditional rabbinical dress apart from the Polish fur hat, which was popular up to the nineteenth century, and modern rabbinical dress is based on the black Geneva gown and white bands of the Calvinist or Reformed Church.

Illustrations are recognized as the most important feature of any book on costume, but survivals from ancient times are largely

[7] See p. 20   [8] See p. 21

fortuitous so that while much is known about Sumerian costume in the third millennium and Assyrian costume in the first millennium BC, there are no pictorial records of Jewish costume during the five centuries before Christ or between AD 300 and 1000.[9] There is a certain amount of early Christian art which is now recognized as being based on Jewish originals, but as the early Christians regarded themselves as the spiritual heirs of the Jews and pictured themselves in the Old Testament scenes found in churches and on Christian manuscripts, the extent to which the original Jewish models have been retained can only be conjectured. The same models remained in use up to the Renaissance, but from the eleventh century onwards scenes from the Passion were being used as vehicles for anti-Jewish propaganda and they provide authentic if caricatured representations of Jews in contemporary dress complete with their beards and Jewish hats. At about the same time Jewish manuscripts illustrated with human figures began to appear, followed in the sixteenth century by the first illustrated printed *Haggadoth* and books of *Minhagim*. The same illustrations sometimes served for many successive editions so that the costume is not necessarily contemporary with the book; but by this time numerous books on travel and costume were being published some of which contain illustrations or descriptions of Jewish costume.

Of particular value are actual examples of Jewish costume a few pieces of which are still to be found in European museums, while in recent years much material from the rapidly disappearing Jewries of North Africa and the Middle East has been preserved in Israel, and there are now some splendid exhibits in the new museums at Jerusalem and Tel-Aviv.

ALFRED RUBENS

[9] The Jewish costume shown in the early Christian mosaics at Ravenna and Rome are believed to be based on much earlier models.

Biblical and Talmudic Periods

FOR A DESCRIPTION of the costume of the Hebrews one naturally turns to the Old Testament. Here, the first apparent difficulty is one of translation since a large number of words describing items of dress in the Hebrew text are given the same equivalent in the English versions. There are, for instance, seven different Hebrew words rendered 'veil' of which four occur in *Isaiah* and the correct translation might be 'shawl', 'wrap', or 'mantle'. In many instances the meaning of a word has been lost but in some cases it is explained by the context and in the later writings one is helped by the corresponding text of the Septuagint and to a certain extent by Josephus.

The evidence of the Bible supported by archaeology leads to the conclusion that the costume of the Hebrews did not differ to any material extent from that worn by the neighbouring peoples. The basic garments were known in Hebrew as the *simlah* or *salmah*, the *ezor* and the *kethoneth*.

The *simlah* was the long roll of cloth, rectangular or shaped, worn as an outer garment by most peoples of Western Asia. It was the Greek *himation* and the Roman *pallium*. It served as a blanket[1] and the Israelites used it in order to carry the dough for their bread and their kneading bowls.[2]

The *ezor* (Arabic *izar*) was the simplest form of dress and although usually translated 'girdle' was a loin cloth. Jeremiah wore it on his loins.[3] When Isaiah removed his *ezor* he was naked[4] and a king is humbled by being made to wear the *ezor*.[5]

The *kethoneth* was another garment in general use. It was the Greek *chiton* and corresponded with the Roman *tunica*. It was a shirt-like garment with long or short sleeves and came down below the knees sometimes to the ankles. It was usually of wool or linen but could be made of skins.[6]

An early example of the *simlah* is seen on a Sumerian priest-god [Plate 1] of about 2250 BC from Ur of the Chaldees, the traditional birthplace of Abraham. It is fringed and worn wrapped round the body. The same garment is seen on a number of scarabs found in Palestine dating from the Hyksos period (*c.* 1670–1570 BC) which is believed to correspond approximately with the time of the Patriarchs and the period during which the Hebrews settled in Egypt.[7]

According to Deuteronomy xxvi:5 'a

[1] Exodus xxii: 27 [2] Exodus xii: 34
[3] Jeremiah xiii: 2 [4] Isaiah xx: 2
[5] Job xii: 18 [6] Genesis iii: 21
[7] Illustrated in *Anatolian Studies*, vi, London 1956

1

wandering Aramaean was my father and he went down into Egypt and sojourned there few in number and there he became a nation, great mighty and prosperous'. If, as the Bible implies, the Hebrews and the Aramaeans (Syrians) were kinsmen it is probable that the Syrian dress shown on Plates 2 and 3 was similar to that worn by the Hebrews. Plate 2 shows the *ezor*. In Plate 3 most of the Semitic envoys from Syria appear to be wearing the *simlah* wrapped round the *kethoneth*. They have the usual pointed Syrian beards and a fillet round the hair. An unusual feature of their dress is the long sleeves.

The oldest monument on which Israelites are represented is the 'black obelisk' of Shalmaneser III (842 BC) in the British Museum. This is divided into five registers of which the second shows Jehu King of Israel paying homage to the Assyrian King. He is followed by four Assyrian court officials after whom come thirteen Israelite porters bearing tribute. They wear over the *kethoneth* a fringed *simlah* draped over the left shoulder with the end flung over the right shoulder. Their dress is distinguished from that of the Assyrians by their pointed caps and sandals with upturned toes. Their beards trimmed to a point are also distinctive. Jehu himself wears the same

1 *SUMER : Ur c. 2250–2040 BC*
[PRIEST-GOD FIGURE] *Oriental Museum, Istanbul*
Wearing kethoneth *and fringed* simlah *which remained the basic costume of the ancient Near East for fifteen hundred years.*

2 *EGYPT : c. 1450 BC*
[TOMB PAINTING] *Detail. British Museum*
Foreigners bearing gifts wearing Syrian dress. The standing figure holding his infant son has the typical pointed Syrian beard and wears a long-sleeved kethoneth *with tassels attached to its hem, the centre ones being blue and brown.*

3 *EGYPT : Thebes c. 1450 BC*
[TOMB PAINTING] *British Museum*
Semitic envoys from Retenu in Syria bringing gifts to Egypt. With one exception they wear a long-sleeved kethoneth *around which is wrapped the* simlah. *All the garments are white and are edged with blue and red. Syrian style beards and hair fillets.*

cap and apparently a fringed *kethoneth* down to his ankles without a *simlah*. There are slight traces of a girdle and he probably had tassels hanging from his waist like those worn by the Assyrian official who follows him. The Assyrians are shown with the *simlah* draped in a different manner and the King wears a special head-dress and tassels attached to cords suspended from the waist [Plate 4].

These reliefs by themselves do not supply conclusive evidence of Israelite costume because on the same monument the sculptor shows other peoples of Western Asia wearing identical dress; in the first register, Sua the Gilzanite is shown in the costume worn by Jehu and in the same attitude, but the same costume is seen on prisoners from the Israelite city of Astartu (Ashtaroth?) after its capture by Tiglath-Pileser III (745–727 BC).[8] There is therefore a strong possibility that it is authentic Israelite costume, although it almost certainly was not exclusive to them. It is different from the costume of the Judaean prisoners who are seen being led away after the capture of Lachish by Sennacherib in 701 BC [Plates 8–9]. These wear a short-sleeved full length *kethoneth*, are bareheaded and have closely trimmed beards, while the beards of the Israelites are more pointed

in the Syrian manner.

There is no mention of head-dress in the Bible in pre-exilic times but there are other Assyrian reliefs in the British Museum showing gangs of Semitic prisoners wearing caps.

Women wore the *simlah* [Plate 8] but theirs could be distinguished in some way from the men's, possibly by its shape or colour.[9] They used cosmetics[10] and there are many references to ornaments, bracelets, earrings and rings. This quotation from Isaiah indicates how wide was the choice:

'The Lord will take away the bravery of their tinkling ornaments about their feet and their cauls and their round tires like the moon. The chains and the bracelets and the mufflers. The bonnets and the ornaments of the legs and the headbands and the tablets and the earrings. The rings and nose jewels. The changeable suits of apparel and the mantles and the wimples and the crisping pins. The glasses and the fine linen and the hoods and the vails.'[11]

Shoes are frequently mentioned in the Old Testament, the ordinary Hebrew term being *nealim* which in the Septuagint is usually rendered *hupodemata* but sometimes *sandalia*. *Hupodema* originally denoted a sandal but was later applied to the Roman *calceus* (a shoe which covered the whole foot).

[8] British Museum 118908   [9] Deuteronomy xxii: 5
[10] Ezekiel xxiii:40   2 Kings ix:30   [11] Isaiah iii:18–23

The materials used for clothing were linen, wool and skins. The Hebrew word for cotton, *karpas*, from the Persian *kirpas* is found only in the Book of Esther.

Brides wore special dress and both bride and bridegroom wore jewels or ornaments.[12]

The Bible mentions three distinctions for Jewish dress: the wearing of tassels *(tsitsith)*; the treatment of the hair *(peoth)* and the law of *shaatnez*. This last, found in Deuteronomy xxii:11, was a prohibition against the mixture of wool and linen, but as it did not apply to the High Priest's girdle nor to *tsitsith*[13] the objection does not seem to have been on moral grounds and one sees in it an early example of a sumptuary law; it is comparable with Inca law whereby vicuna wool was reserved for the ruling classes.[14]

There are two references in the Old Testament to the wearing of tassels. The more specific one is Numbers xv:38: 'Speak unto the children of Israel and bid them to make a tassel *(tsitsith)* on the corners of their garments throughout their generations and to put on it a twined cord of blue *(techeleth)*'. The other is Deuteronomy xxii:12: 'You shall make for yourself twisted cords *(gedilim)*[15] on the four corners of your wrap *(kesuth)* with which you cover yourself.' Here the garment referred to is evidently the *simlah*, with which *kesuth* is synonymous, as opposed to general articles of clothing mentioned in Numbers, which would require a different kind of appendage; *gedilim* may have a different meaning from *tsitsith* a word which implies a flower-like form.[16] Another difference in the two texts is that the passage in Deuteronomy does not specify any colour.

According to tradition, *techeleth* represented sky-blue[17]; it was made from chemicals mixed with the juice of a mollusc (Heb. *hhallazona*) similar to the *murex brandaris* which produced the rare Tyrian purple dye ultimately reserved for royalty. These shellfish were so much sought after that they were almost exterminated; by Talmudic times the *techeleth* dye had become unobtainable.[18]

There were in fact two kinds of tassel in common use in Western Asia. One with three threads, which may be the *tsitsith*, is particularly associated with the Philistines [Plate 7]

12 Isaiah lxi:10 Jeremiah ii:32
13 Talmud B. *Menahoth* 6a and 39b
14 Compare also the specific statement by Josephus: 'let none of you wear raiment of wool and linen for that is reserved for the priests alone'. (Loeb ed. 1930 *Jewish Antiquities* iv:211.)
15 Babylonian *gidlu* = a string
16 See Isaiah xxvii:6 and xxviii:1, 4
17 The Septuagint renders it *huakinthos* i.e. hyacinth or blue.
18 T. B. *Menahoth* 42b and 44a and see C. E. Pellew, *Dyes and Dyeing*, London, 1928, 26–9

4

but it is also found on Syrian dress in Egypt and is perhaps a stylized form of flower with the same magic properties as the lotus blossom. The other tassel, the *gedilim* or twisted cord, was probably similar to that seen in Plate 6 attached to the corner of a *simlah*.

Among the Assyrians this type of tassel on cords suspended from the waist was a symbol of rank worn by the King and his chief officers and it also no doubt had some religious significance. In the palace at Khorsabad built by the Assyrian King Sargon II (721–705 BC) there were reliefs showing subject people, believed to be Anatolians or Phrygians, with various kinds of tassel attached to the corners of their tunics [Plate 11].

The special treatment of the hair and the wearing of side locks *(peoth)* is based on Leviticus xix:27: 'Ye shall not round the corners *(peoth)* of your heads neither shalt thou mar the corners of thy beard.'

Here again there is no evidence from antiquity that this was a Jewish custom, side locks being in fact the characteristic feature of certain other peoples, particularly the Libyans [see Plate 5] and Cretans. The Hebrews shown on the Assyrian reliefs are without *peoth* or *tsitsith* but this may be due to the fact that they came into use at a later date or

4 *ASSYRIA: 841 BC*
[ISRAELITES CARRYING TRIBUTE] *Detail from 'Black Obelisk'. British Museum 118885*
Each wears a kethoneth *with fringed hem over which is draped a* simlah *the tasseled end of which is thrown over the left shoulder. Pointed cap, sandals with upturned toes, and pointed beard.*

5 *EGYPT: 1180 BC*
[LIBYAN] *Foreign prisoner tile*
Cairo Museum
He wears side-locks and his body is tattooed.

6 *PALESTINE: c. 750 BC*
[STATUETTE] *Jordan Archaeological Museum*
Aramaean deity (?) holding in his left hand a lotus stalk. Over a short-sleeved kethoneth *with girdle he wears a fringed* simlah *the corners of which are bound and terminate in tassels. He has side locks, a short square beard and his hair is worn in a fillet. Illustrated London News 18 February 1950. R.D. Barnett, 'Four Sculptures from Amman' in Annual of Department of Antiquities of Jordan, I, Amman, 1951.*

7 *EGYPT: c. 1180 BC*
[PHILISTINE] *Foreign prisoner tile*
Cairo Museum
He has a tassel in the shape of a trefoil attached to the projecting edge of his tunic.

6

5

7

because the sculptor did not take his figures from life.

A change in the traditional costume of the Bible must have occurred in the time of Zephaniah (*c.* 630 BC) to produce his outburst: 'I will punish the princes and the king's children and all such as are clothed with strange apparel'.[19] This probably marks a trend towards Iranian costume which was similar to that worn by the Lydians and Phrygians, its chief characteristics being sewed garments, a coat of varying length with sleeves, riding trousers and as a rule, boots, leggings, cloak and a high cap of felt.

This remained the basic costume of the Persian empire up to the Islamic period and it had probably become the accepted Jewish dress by the time of the return to Palestine under Cyrus in 538 BC. Its influence is seen to an outstanding degree in the embroidered coat, linen trousers and mitre of the High Priest, the most completely documented piece of Jewish costume of ancient times. The description given by Josephus[20] is particularly valuable because as a member of the priestly family he spoke from personal knowledge; it differs from the one given in Exodus xxviii and shows how the costume gradually developed. Josephus describes the head-dress of the High Priest as a cap *(pilos)*, with another of blue embroidery over it, surmounted by a golden crown in three tiers with a golden calyx sprouting from it.[21] This is comparable with the elaborate Parthian diadem worn by Persian royalty, officials and gods which in Sassanid times became a true crown with a mystic meaning attached to every detail.

Persian influence is seen also in the dress of the 'Three Children in the Furnace' described in Daniel iii:21: 'Then these men were bound in their coats *(sarbalehon)*, their hosen *(pateshehon)*, and their hats *(karbelathehon)* and their other garments'. The three Aramaic words describing their dress are obscure in origin and their meaning has been much debated.

In Talmudic times the *sarbal* was a cloak and by the Middle Ages it had acquired special importance for prayer.[22] I see no reason for not adopting this meaning in Daniel and the Talmudic meaning for *patesh* —leg covering fastened at the hips—is equally

[19] Zephaniah i:8.
[20] Loeb ed., 1930 *Jewish Antiquities* iii:150–80.
[21] cf. Ecclesiastes xlv:12: 'a crown of gold upon the mitre'.
[22] Jastrow also gives the alternative translation 'Persian trousers' but generally a cloak is indicated, e.g. 'Abaye goes out in a worn *sarbal*'. (T. B. *Mo'ed Katan* 23a.)

acceptable. The word *karbela* means 'cock's comb' which seems to refer to the Persian hat of this shape, the *kyrbasia*, which came into fashion during the Achaemenid period (546–330 BC).

It is interesting to find this interpretation of the text translated into picture form on a fourth-century painting from Egypt of the 'Three Children in the Furnace', the only additions being the Coptic roundels on their tunics [Plate 14]. The 'Three Children in the Furnace' and 'Daniel in the Den of Lions' are referred to in the earliest known Christian prayers as instances of deliverance through divine intervention and they were two of the most popular subjects for the designs on Christian sarcophagi. These are perhaps some of the designs which according to art historians have been borrowed from Jewish sources. They could well be contemporary with the Book of Daniel which was written in the second century BC.

It cannot be assumed from the dress described in the Book of Daniel that Persian fashions were in vogue among Jews everywhere at that period. This may have been true of Babylon but from the time of Alexander the Jews of Palestine and Egypt were subject to very strong Hellenizing influences.

During the third century BC under the Ptolemies they had begun to adopt Greek names and when they came under the Seleucids after the capture of Jerusalem by Antiochus III in 198 BC the Hellenistic influences were intensified. The confirmation by Antiochus III of the right to live in accordance with their ancestral laws may have permitted some distinction in their dress, but Hellenism had by then taken such a firm hold that Greek dress must have become the normal attire at least for the aristocracy. However, when Jason seized power as high priest in 175 BC and turned Jerusalem into a Greek city his attempt to introduce the *petasos*, the Greek broad-brimmed hat associated with Hermes, was strongly opposed.[23]

But whatever resistance to Hellenism there may have been in Palestine, the Jews in Alexandria, the most important Jewish centre in classical times, came completely under Greek influence, and as Tcherikover points out the Septuagint was made not for Gentiles but for the benefit of Jews who could not understand Hebrew. It is not difficult to accept the modern view that versions of the Septuagint appeared in Alexandria with illustrations and that these are the

[23] 2 Maccabees, iv:12.

C

8

sources for much early Christian art. Certainly Plate 19, part of a mosaic from the Church of S. Vitale at Ravenna, provides a credible picture of Alexandrian Jews in pre-Christian times.

In Palestine under the Hasmonean kings Greek influence remained predominant and by New Testament times Greek dress seems to have been generally adopted. The usual garment worn by Jesus and the apostles was the *colobium*,[24] a long tunic in one piece with three openings for the head and arms over which was draped the *himation* with *tsitsith* attached to its four corners.[25] In the Greek New Testament *tsitsith* are called *kraspeda* or borders and it was after touching this part of Jesus' *himation* that the woman suffering from a haemorrhage was cured.[26] The *tsitsith* were regarded as a symbol of orthodoxy and Jesus attacked the scribes and Pharisees for wearing excessively long ones.

The *colobium* was similar to the more modern *dalmatica* except that the latter had very ample sleeves. Both garments were usually decorated with two bands known as *clavi* running from the shoulder to the hem. They were usually purple in colour with one or two bands of the same colour on the sleeves. According to Epiphanius (*c.* 315–402), one

8–9 *PALESTINE: c. 700 BC*
[JUDAEAN PRISONERS FROM LACHISH]
British Museum 124908–10
Details from reliefs showing the capture of the Judaean city of Lachish by Sennacherib in 700 BC. The Judaean men wear short-sleeved kethoneth, *are barefoot and have short trimmed beards. The women wear a* simlah *with a plain border over a plain* kethoneth.

10 *MESOPOTAMIA: Third century AD*
[THE HIGH PRIEST AND HIS ATTENDANTS] *Fresco*
Dura Europos Synagogue
The High Priest is labelled 'Aaron' in Greek but his costume bears little relation to that described in Exodus *or the later version given by Josephus and is the costume of Persian royalty.*[27]
The attendants are dressed in belted tunics and Persian trousers.
Kraeling Plate 60
Reproduced by kind permission of Yale University Press.

[24] John xix:23.
[25] The *himation* or *pallium* should not be confused with the *toga* which was reserved for Roman aristocracy and freemen.
[26] Matthew ix:20; see also xiv:36; xxiii:5   Mark vi:56 Luke viii:44
[27] When Jonathan Maccabaeus was appointed high priest he was presented by Alexander Balas with the royal gold buckle together with purple robes and a gold crown (I. Maccabees x:20; x:89; xiv:44).

9

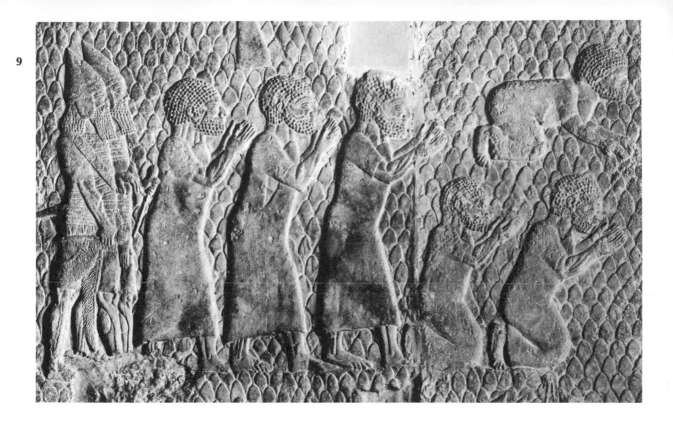

10

of the Church fathers, it was to these *clavi* that Jesus was referring in Matthew xxiii:5 when he said (of the scribes and Pharisees) 'they make broad their phylacteries'.[28] This is much more acceptable than the usual interpretation that the text refers to *tephillin*, which by their nature do not lend themselves to being made broad. The *dalmatica* with *clavi* is the dress in which the early Christians are shown in the catacombs at Rome and it is also assigned to Jews in the early Christian mosaics. Indeed it seems that in early Christian times Jews and Christians were indistinguishable and Justin, one of the fathers of the Church, in a dialogue with Trypho the Jew written in the middle of the second century says: 'You are not recognized among the rest of men by any other mark than your fleshly circumcision'.[29] In fact the Ravenna mosaics provide evidence that some of the early Christians wore *tsitsith*. Examples are to be found on the cupola of the sixth-century Baptistery of the Arians, and in the groups of Christian martyrs in the sixth-century Basilica of S. Apollinare Nuovo [Plate 17]. They are also worn by the Apostle Matthew on a mosaic of the same period in the Church of S. Vitale. Nevertheless the custom of wearing *tsitsith* must have been abandoned by Christians at an early date for, according to the Talmud, they were a means of identifying a Jew[30] and they are significantly absent on all traditional portraits of Jesus. It is interesting to note that the Christian *tsitsith* seen at Ravenna consisting of a pair of cords are similar to those worn by the followers of Bar Kochba.[31]

In the Midrash, the Mishnah and the Talmud the words used to describe dress are almost entirely Greek or Latin terms transliterated into Hebrew and most of the garments are of Greek, Roman or Iranian origin. We learn for instance that 'Raba goes out in a new Roman red tunic'.[32]

In the following list of the principal garments mentioned in these works, the first sixteen are designated in the Talmud as essential.[33]

[28] See Goodenough, ix:171. Epiphanius also believed that the *kraspeda* were *tsitsith*.
[29] See Parkes, 119 and 274.
[30] T. B. *Menahoth* 43a.
[31] Illustrated in Y. Yadin *The Finds from the Bar-Kokhba Period*, Jerusalem, 1963.
[32] T. B. *Mo'ed Katan*, 23a
[33] T. B. *Shabbat* 120a. T. J. *Shabbat* xvi:5. The essential garments numbered eighteen, counting pairs as two. The two lists vary slightly and are here combined.

	GREEK EQUIVALENT	LATIN EQUIVALENT	DESCRIPTION
MIQTORIN		*amictorium*	wrapped garment, cloak or scarf
UNQELAI	*anacholos*		under-tunic
PHUNDA		*funda*	money belt
QOLOB	*kolobus*	*colobium*	linen tunic
HHALUQ			shirt
APPILION		*pallium*	*pallium*
MAAPORETH		*mappa*	napkin; apron
SABHRIQIN	*subrichion*	*subucula*	woman's tunic
MINALIM			shoes
IMPILAYOTH		*impilia*	socks; felt shoes
APHRIQIN		*bracae*	trousers or breeches
PARGOD		*paragauda*	bordered garment
HHAGORAH			girdle
KOBHA SHEBEROSHO			head covering
SUDAR SHEBETSAVARO	*soudarion*	*sudarium*	kerchief for the neck
SUDAR SHEAL ZEROTHAV	*soudarion*	*sudarium*	kerchief for the arm
ISTIKHARION	*sticharion*		short-sleeved jacket
ITSTELA; ISTELA	*stole*	*stola*	shawl; *tallith*
BUROS		*birrus*	rectangular cloak or cape with hood attached
BALNERI		*balnearia*	bath clothes
DALMATIQON		*dalmatica*	
TOGA		*toga*	
KALMUS	*chlamus*	*chlamys*	cloak
SAGOS; SAGUM	*sagos*	*sagum*	coarse woollen blanket or mantle
SANDAL	*sandalon*	*sandalium*	sandal
PILION	*pilos*	*pileus*	felt cap
PHALNIS	*phainoles*	*paenula*	cloak or mantle; *cucullus*
PHAMALNIYA		*feminalia*	leggings

11

The mixture of classical and Iranian costume reflected in the foregoing list is illustrated in the frescoes from the third-century synagogue at Dura Europos. Dura, a Roman fortress on the Euphrates frontier, was totally destroyed by the Sassanians in AD 256. Before being incorporated in the Roman Empire it had been a Parthian city and before that had been held by the Seleucids, and its costume as well as its art and architecture display the joint Iranian and Graeco-Roman influences which were the feature of Palmyran culture. The remarkable series of paintings illustrating the Old Testament displays all these elements. The costume presents somewhat of a puzzle since the artist makes no distinction between Jew and heathen. Philistine and Israelite infantry are similarly attired and there is no difference as regards dress between Pharaoh, David and Ahasuerus nor between Moses, Samuel, Ezra and the Prophets of Baal. There are two distinct types of dress: the Graeco-Roman consisting of *dalmatica* or *colobium* with *clavi*, *pallium (himation)* and sandals; and the Iranian, consisting of tunic, trousers and boots or shoes. Both Seyrig and Goodenough question whether the costumes in the exact form shown are contemporary.

11 *ASSYRIA: 722–705 BC*
[PRISONERS OF SARGON II] *From a relief at the Palace of Khorsabad built by Sargon II King of Assyria.*
From Botta
The tailored tunics with double tassels on the corners are not found in Syria or Palestine and the figures probably represent Anatolians or Phrygians.

12 *MESOPOTAMIA: Third century AD*
[MOSES AND THE BURNING BUSH] *Fresco*
Dura Europos Synagogue
Kraeling Plate 76
Moses in yellow dalmatica *with* clavi *and* pallium *decorated with two-pronged marks* (gams). *Instead of the usual sandals he wears high white boots. He has short hair, a moustache and close-cropped beard.*
Reproduced by kind permission of Yale University Press.

13 *PALESTINE: c. 500 BC*
[COSTUME OF THE HIGH PRIEST] *Engraving (modern)*
A reconstruction of the costume described in Exodus xxviii : 9.

12

13

In one or two cases there are signs of *tsit-sith* on the corners of the *pallium* [Plate 18] and most of the Greek costumes have on them the pronged ornaments common during the Hellenistic period and known in Christian tradition as *gams* from their similarity in shape to the Greek letter *gamma*. They are seen on much of the dress in the early mosaics at Ravenna and at S. Maria Maggiore in Rome [Plate 15]. That they were worn by Jews is confirmed by the textiles found recently in the caves used by Bar Kochba.[34]

Other ornaments found on Jewish costume at Ravenna and elsewhere are the round or square patches of material known as *segmentae*. Somewhat similar to these are the roundels which are seen on Jewish dress on Plate 14 and in the fourth-century Exodus paintings at Bagawat in Egypt.[35] These are said to have originated in Syria, but most of those which have survived come from Egypt, having been recovered from Coptic tombs of the 6th–7th century, and they usually have on them some Christian symbolism. I had long hoped to find one with characteristics to indicate that it had been worn by a Jew and eventually a very fine example came to light embroidered with the story of Joseph accompanied by two Hebrew letters [Plate 21].

In a different tradition are the distinctive marks on clothing, indicating the wearer's occupation, which are mentioned in the Talmud.[36] Scholars carried a sign on their head-covering, slaves on their clothes; the tailor carried a needle, the scribe a pen at his ear, the money-changer a coin, the carpenter a chip of wood, the weaver and comber a woollen thread and so on. This was perhaps the means whereby the different trades were identified in the Great Synagogue at Alexandria where, we are told, they remained in separate groups.[37]

The custom for Jewish married women to have their head covered is of considerable antiquity. In the Mishnah it is described as a 'Jewish Ordinance'[38] but its Biblical origin based on Numbers v:18 is questionable. In Talmudic times it was considered immodest for a married woman to stir outside the house without a covering on her head although a work basket was considered sufficient,[39] and if a Jewish woman wore her hair uncovered it was assumed that she was a virgin.[40] To the outside world a woman with her head completely covered was stamped as a Jewess.

[34] Illustrated in Yadin, *op. cit.* [35] Illustrated in Fakhry
[36] T. J. *Shabbat* 1:3 [37] T. B. *Sukkah,* 51b
[38] Mishnah, *Kethuboth* vii:6 [39] T. B. *Kethuboth* 72b
[40] T. B. *Berakoth* 24a; Mishnah, *Kethuboth* ii:10

For this we have the authority of Tertullian (*c.* AD 155–222), one of the fathers of the Christian Church, who wrote: 'Among the Jews, so usual is it for their women to have the head veiled that they may thereby be recognized'.[41] Christian matrons were also supposed to keep their heads veiled but in his *De Virginibus Velandis* Tertullian complains that many of them merely bound their heads with woollen bands while others wore small linen coifs instead of covering their heads from ear to ear. Tertullian also denounced the wearing of wigs.

Jewish women wore wigs in Talmudic times[42] but it was much later that the custom grew up for women to cut their hair on marriage and to cover their shorn locks with a wig. This was regarded as a novelty and as such was denounced by the rabbis;[43] nevertheless by some curious quirk the wig or *sheitel* as it is known in Yiddish became in time the prerogative of the ultra-orthodox. Cutting the bride's hair was in fact a pagan custom practised in ancient Greece where the bride's hair was dedicated to the goddess. The same custom existed in South-East Russia, Prussia and Sicily.[44]

If women were obliged to cover their heads there was no obligation for men to do so. All the men shown in the Dura Synagogue except the High Priest are bareheaded and the Talmud contains no requirement that the head should be covered during prayer. There seems to have been no absolute rule in the matter and probably the best exposition of Jewish practice is that given by St Paul:

'A man who keeps his head covered when he prays or prophesies brings shame on his head; a woman, on the contrary, brings shame on her head if she prays or prophesies bare-headed: it is as bad as if her head were shaved. If a woman is not to wear a veil she might as well have her hair cut off; but if it is a disgrace for her to be cropped and shaved, then she should wear a veil. A man has no need to cover his head, because man is the image of God, and the mirror of his glory, whereas woman reflects the glory of man.'[45]

The *sudarium* or kerchief worn by Jesus[46]

41 'Apud Judaeos tam solenne est feminis eorum velamen capitis ut inde noscantur' *De Corona Militis*, iv
42 T.B. *Nazir* 28b; *Sanhedrin* 112a; *Arakin* 7b
43 Moses Sofer of Presburg (1763–1839), a great authority on Jewish law, in his will expressly forbade any of the women of his family to wear a wig. Akiba Joseph Schlessinger, in his book *Lev Ha-Ivri*, comments on this passage in the will and cites many other authorities who forbade the wig. Opposition had started in the 16th–17th centuries when women began to wear a wig without a kerchief over it. The objection was on moral grounds and also through fear of novelties and new fashions. (Based on a communication from Rabbi Dr Solomon B. Freehof.)
44 T.H. Gaster, 106
45 I. Corinthians xi:4–7. For a full consideration of the question of covering the head see Abrahams, *Jewish Life*, 300–2.
46 John xx:7

14

was used by Jews in Talmudic times and a special benediction was recited when it was donned in the morning.[47] Among the Romans one was worn round the neck and another over the left shoulder or forearm corresponding with the two types mentioned in the Talmud, neither of which seems to have served as a head covering.

Tephillin consist of two small leather boxes attached by leather thongs, one to the forehead the other to the left arm [see Plate 22]. Each contains four passages from the Pentateuch. They are now worn by orthodox Jews for morning prayers but in Talmudic times scholars wore them throughout the day in accordance with rabbinical precept. Their use is based on Exodus xii:9, 16 and Deuteronomy vi:8, xi:18 but the critical view is that these passages merely prove that the Hebrews originally wore amulets or tattoo marks on the forehead and hands and that in this respect they followed the practices of certain other Mediterranean peoples.[48] For this reason they are rejected by Reform Jews. They are not mentioned in the Old Testament and the supposed reference in Matthew xxiii:5 is questionable for the reasons given above. They are however referred to by Josephus[49] and some

14 *EGYPT: Sixth century AD*
[THE THREE CHILDREN IN THE FURNACE] *Wall painting From Wadi Sarga, Egypt. British Museum*
The three children wear a Persian hat, (kyrbasia), a cloak fastened in front, belted tunic with roundels near the lower edge and long Persian leggings.

15 *ITALY: Rome 432–440 AD*
[ABRAHAM AND SARAH] *S. Maria Maggiore, Rome From Wilpert.*
Part of a mosaic illustrating the story of Abraham and the Three Angels (Genesis xviii:1–3). Abraham wears pale yellow colobium with clavi and a pallium decorated with gams. Sarah has a white under-tunic of which only the tight white sleeves are visible from the elbows downwards; an orange dalmatica with clavi and on her head a white coif indicating her married status.

16 *PALESTINE: Sixth century AD*
[THE SACRIFICE OF ISAAC] *Mosaic detail Beth-Alpha Synagogue, Israel*
Abraham wearing shoes is in a colobium with clavi and long sleeves with bands round the cuffs.

[47] T. B. *Berakoth* 60b
[48] Terracotta prophylactic masks dating from about 500 BC, with frontlets between the eyes, have been found in graves at Tharros in North Africa. There is an example in the British Museum and several are illustrated in Cintas.
[49] Loeb ed. 1930 *J.A.* iv:213. A detailed study of the nature and history of *tephillin* will be found in *The Jewish Encyclopedia* s.v. 'Phylacteries'.

15

16

17

examples dating from the first century AD were recently discovered by Professor Yadin in the Bar Kochba caves.

By the second century AD the *pallium* or *himation* was regarded in Rome as the attribute of learned men. By the fourth century it had ceased to be a common article of dress and was retained as an official garment for certain high officers. It was then worn folded two or three times, reducing its width to about eighteen inches. The removal of the surplus material finally reduced it to a scarf or stole. The fact that it was one of the garments worn by Jesus invested it with some degree of sanctity, and the ecclesiastical *pallium*, ultimately reduced to a single strip of cloth or silk, is still worn by high dignitaries of the Christian church.

By a somewhat similar sequence of events the *pallium* worn by Jews must have developed into the modern *tallith*. In Talmudic times it was still essentially an attribute of scholars who wore it over a long undergarment (Heb. *hhaluk*) which covered the body down to the feet.[50] The *tallith* had threads attached to its corners forming *tsitsith*, but there were two schools of thought as to their correct number and colour, Beth Shammai maintaining that there

17 *ITALY: Ravenna sixth century AD*
[CHRISTIAN MARTYRS] *Mosaic*
S. Apollinare Nuovo
Two of them have a double thread (tsitsith) *attached to the corners of their* pallia.

18 *MESOPOTAMIA: Third century AD*
[TSITSITH] *Sketch from fresco. Dura Europos Synagogue*
Kraeling Figure 22
Detail from 'Moses and the Crossing of the Red Sea' (Kraeling Plates 52–3) showing stylized form of tsitsith *on the tip of Moses'* pallium.
Reproduced by kind permission of Yale University Press.

19 *ITALY: Ravenna sixth century AD*
[ALEXANDRIAN JEWS] *Mosaic. S. Vitale*
A group of Alexandrian Jews of the first or second century BC representing Aaron and the twelve tribes of Israel.

20 *GERMANY: Eighteenth century*
TALLITH *with gold brocade centre and corners*
Jewish Museum, London.

[50] T. B. *Baba Bathra* 58a and 98a *Shabbat* 10a

18

19

20

21

should be four threads of white wool and four of blue, Beth Hillel that there should be two of each colour. This difference of opinion may be a clue to the original distinction between *tsitsith* and *gedilim*, while the lack of any absolute rule about colour can be attributed to the disappearance of the *hhalazona*, the mollusc from which by tradition the *techeleth* dye was obtained.[51] The religious significance of the *tsitsith* was recognized by the special benediction recited over them as part of the ordinary routine of dressing[52] but the *tallith* is not one of the essential garments listed in the Talmud.[53] Etymologically it seems to be the same word as *stole* and it is the *stole* rather than the *pallium* which is its counterpart in the Christian church.[54]

The modern *tallith*, [see Plates 20, 22–3], a prayer shawl for males who have reached the age of thirteen[55], is woven of wool or silk, in white, with black or blue stripes at the ends. The silk ones vary in size from 54 to 96 inches in length and from 36 to 72 inches in width; the woollen *tallith* is larger, sometimes reaching to the ankle, and is made of two lengths sewed together, the stitching being covered with a narrow silk ribbon. A ribbon or a band woven with silver or gold

21 *EGYPT: Sixth century AD*
[THE STORY OF JOSEPH] *Wool on linen*
Stadtisches Museum, Trier, West Germany
Roundel from a tunic presumably worn by a Jew on account of the two Hebrew letters which form part of the design.

22 *HOLLAND: Seventeenth century*
[MAN DRESSED FOR PRAYERS] *Engraving*
Wearing tallith *and* tephillin. *Above:* tephillin *for the arm and for the head. Sephardi synagogue at Amsterdam in background.*

23 *RUSSIA: Nineteenth century*
KARAITE TALLITH AND BAG. *From the* Jewish Encyclopædia.

[51] T. B. *Menahoth* 41b [52] T. B. *Berakoth* 60b [53] See p. 16
[54] Although this conclusion seems inescapable to me it is not apparently accepted by Church historians. See *The Catholic Encyclopaedia*, New York, 1912. xiv:302.
[55] In some communities it is worn only after marriage.

22

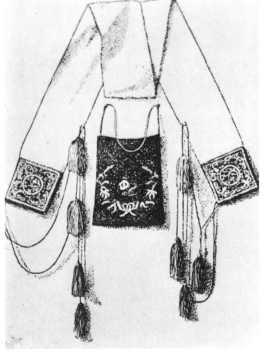

23

thread is sometimes sewn along the top edge where it touches the neck. This is usually called the *ata* and according to Goldstein and Dresdner, who reproduce a number of examples, the traditional design is Spanish and of Sephardi origin. This would account for the alternative name, *spania*, by which the band is known. From each of the four corners of the *tallith* hang the *tsitsith* consisting of four threads looped to form eight which may be blue or white in colour.[56]

Some time after the *tallith* had fallen into disuse as an article of clothing its place was taken by the *arba kanphoth* in order to fulfil the requirements of Numbers xv:38 and Deuteronomy xxii:12. The *arba kanphoth* (four corners) or *tallith katan* is first mentioned in the code of Jacob ben Asher *c.* 1350. It normally consists of a rectangular piece of cloth usually of wool, about three feet long and one foot wide with an aperture for the head. To its four corners are attached *tsitsith* [see Plate 189]. Among orthodox Jews it is still worn by males from childhood as an undergarment throughout the day but in the ghettoes it was sometimes worn as an outer garment [see Plate 167] and occasionally, perhaps for Sabbath use, it was richly embroidered [see Plate 199].

AUTHORITIES: I. Abrahams; S. Bertman; M. P. E. Botta; F. G. Bratton; *Brit. Mus. Cat. of Ivory Carvings*; *Brit. Mus. Guide to early Christian Antiquities*; A. Brüll; E. A. W. Budge; P. Cintas; T. Ehrenstein; *Encyc. Biblica*; *Encyc. Judaica*; Ahmed Fakhry; P. R. Garrucci; E. R. Goodenough; C. H. Gordon; O. R. Gurney; L. & J. Heuzey; U. Hölscher; M. G. Houston; *International Standard Bible Encyc.*; *Interpreter's Bible*; M. Jastrow; *Jewish Encyc.*; A. F. Kendrick; E. G. Kraeling; S. Krauss; H. F. Lutz; C. F. Morey; *New Schaff-Herzog Encyc.*; H. Norris; A. Parrot; R. Pfister & L. Bellinger; J. S. Parkes; J. B. Pritchard; A. Rosenzweig; D. Talbot Rice; J. P. Richter & A. C. Taylor; S. Schemel; H. Seyrig; E. L. Sukenik; V. Tcherikover; R. de Vaux; J. Wilpert; C. L. Woolley. *(See Bibliography)*

[56] No medieval *tallith* has survived but most Jewish museums can show examples of more modern ones, some of them richly embroidered. The Victoria and Albert Museum has pieces of seventeenth century Italian needlepoint silk lace from a *tallith*. (V & A 187–1874 etc.)

The Eastern World

China

Jewish settlements in China were associated with the silk trade between China and Rome and there is every reason to believe that their origins go back at least to the first century of the Christian era. According to their own traditions the Jews entered China during the Han Dynasty (206 BC–AD 221) or more exactly during the reign of Han Ming-Ti (AD 58–76). Graetz connects their arrival with the persecution of the Jews in Persia in AD 231. The original communities were probably continually recruiting new members from Persia, Turkestan and India and Elkan Adler found that their customs were similar to those observed by the Jews of Bokhara. The community at K'ai-Fêng the capital of Honan was the last to disappear. Some of their religious practices, such as the observance of the New Moon Festival, indicate a pre-Talmudic origin. In the synagogue during the reading of the Law the minister covered his face with a transparent veil of gauze in memory of Moses, who came down from the mountain with his face covered—a custom unknown elsewhere but mentioned by St Paul as being well established in his time.[1] The *tallith* was not worn, but for *Simchat Torah* (Feast of

Tabernacles) a red silk scarf was draped over the right shoulder and tied under the left arm. As was customary in the East shoes were removed before entering the synagogue, except by the rabbi who alone wore blue shoes and sat on an elevated position beneath a large red satin umbrella. The men wore blue caps in synagogue and the women had to remove their headscarves.

The Jesuit priest, Matteo Ricci, who talked to one of the Chinese Jews in 1605, described him as a Jew in religion, race and features, but the sketches made at K'ai-Fêng a century later by Jean Domenge, another Jesuit, show that the Jews he met were indistinguishable from the Chinese [see Plate 27].

Renewed interest in the Chinese Jews has been aroused in recent years following the discovery of clay tomb figures of the T'ang Dynasty (AD 618–907) with semitic features. These figures form part of the *Ming Chi* which were buried with the dead in accordance with the Chinese practice to provide the deceased with the services to which he was accustomed in his lifetime. Most of them come from around Ch'ang-An, the Western capital, an important centre for foreign

[1] 2 Corinthians iii:14

D

24

trade and situated close to the Jewish settlement at K'ai-Fêng. The tombs in which they were found date between AD 683 and 728.

William Charles White, formerly Bishop of Honan and later Professor of Chinese Studies at the University of Toronto, who lived for twenty-five years at K'ai-Fêng and devoted much of his life to the study of the Chinese Jews and the careful documentation of their history, was convinced that some of these figures represented Jews. This view is supported by Mrs Mahler and Signore Prodan. After examining photographs of figurines in the collections of Mr Frank Caro (C. T. Loo Collection), The Royal Ontario Museum, The Seattle Art Museum and Mrs Brenda Seligman, I have selected, as most likely to represent Jews, the figures with long pointed hats [see Plates 24 & 26]. This hat appears to be the Persian *kalansuwa* and when accompanied by a *caftan* and a corded belt the costume seems to correspond with that worn by Persian Jews (see below). The pedlar with his pack [Plate 24] bears a striking resemblance to the Jewish pedlars of more modern times carrying on their age-old occupation.

AUTHORITIES: E. N. Adler; J. Finn; A. H. Godbey; C. Hentze; R. L. Hobson; *Jewish Encyc.*; J. G. Mahler; M. Prodan; J. Tobar; W. C. White. *(See Bibliography)*

24 *CHINA: c. 618–907*
[POTTERY TOMB FIGURE] *Pedlar in Persian hat and* caftan
T'ang Dynasty (618–907)
C. T. Loo Collection

25 *TURKEY: 1568*
MEDICO GIUDEO. *Etching*
From the Italian edition of De Nicolay
Rubens (ii) 1871
Portrait of Moses Hamon, physician to Sulaiman The Magnificent (1520–66), in the tall hat worn by the Sephardim and short-sleeved caftan.
According to the author 'insteede of a yeallow Tulbant very neere like unto the Jewish nation (he wore) a high topped cappe died of redde scarlet'.

26 *CHINA: c. 618–907*
[POTTERY TOMB FIGURE] *Rug merchant in Persian hat,* caftan *and girdle*
T'ang Dynasty (618–907)
Collection of Mrs B. Seligman

27 *CHINA: 1723*
[CHINESE JEWS READING FROM THE TORAH] *From a sketch by J. Domenge made in 1723*
From Tobar
By this period all differences in dress to distinguish them from the native Chinese had disappeared.

. Medico . Giudeo .

25

26

27

28

Under Islam

From the rise of Islam during the seventh century a great deal of material emerges, much of it confusing, about the special clothing which the *Dhimmis*, the non-Believers, had to wear under Moslem rule. The need to distinguish non-Muslims did not arise until the Arabs with their lower cultural background began to adopt the fashions of the newly converted towns-people, and the first restrictions are believed to have been introduced during the eighth century under the Caliph Umar II—although the 'covenant of Umar' often cited is now regarded as spurious.

The frequent repetition and the lack of uniformity in the Dress Regulations reflect the weakness of the Caliphate after the ninth century and the degree of enforcement no doubt varied in different parts of the empire.

In 849 the Caliph al-Mutawakkil ordered Christians and other non-Believers to wear a yellow Persian mantle, *(tailasân)*, a belt of cord *(zunnâr)*,[2] to fix two balls behind their saddles and to use wooden stirrups only. If they wore the Persian hat, the *kalansuwa (qalansuva)*, they were restricted to certain colours and two buttons of a different colour had to be attached to it; if they wore a

28 *CHINA: 1851*
[CHINESE JEW] *Drawing*
From Illustrated London News *13 December 1851*
Portrait of one of the two Chinese Jews who accompanied missionaries to Shanghai.

29 *TURKEY: 1568*
MERCANTE GIUDEO. *(Cloth Merchant). Etching*
From the Italian edition of De Nicolay
Rubens (ii) 1874
In the turban worn by the native Jews. According to the author the Jews of Turkey wore long garments like those of the other people of the Levant and as a distinction, a yellow turban.

30-31 *TURKEY: Constantinople 1618*
A JEW AT CONSTANTINOPLE. *Male and female figures*
Drawings dated 1618
British Museum Add. Ms. 23880
The man, bearded, in the typical tall hat worn by the Sephardim, the woman wearing an unusual hat.

---

[2] According to Tritton the word in its plural form, *zunnarat*, which came into Arabic from Aramaic and Greek, became so closely identified with non-Muslims that it is used in modern Arabic to describe the Jews' side locks *(peoth)*.

Mercante   *Giudeo*

29

30

31

turban it had to be yellow. This is the first mention of special colours for non-Muslims or of a badge, although at first this last mark of distinction applied only to their slaves, who were required to fix two patches of cloth on their outer garment and of a different colour to it. Four years later all non-Believers were ordered to wear the badge in the form of two patches of yellow cloth. These patches were perhaps the roundels commonly worn on tunics in the Eastern Mediterranean and already referred to above.

In 1004 the mad Caliph of Egypt, al-Hakim, in order to annoy his enemies, the Abbasids, ordered non-Muslims to wear black turbans like theirs and later he decreed that all their clothing should be black. He also required Jews to wear suspended from their neck a block of wood carved to represent the golden calf while Christians were obliged to display an enormous iron cross.

At the end of the twelfth century AD Jewish converts to Islam were required to wear blue clothes[3] with very wide long sleeves and long veils instead of turbans.

By the fourteenth century, under the Mameluks, the distinctive colours were

32 *TURKEY: Adrianople 1568*
DONNA GIUDEA D'ANDRINOPOLI. *Etching*
From the Italian edition of De Nicolay
Rubens (ii) 1003
She is heavily veiled but a small portion of her hair is uncovered.

33 *TURKEY: c. 1650*
FEMME JUIFVE. *Engraving*
From G. de la Chapelle Recueil De Divers Portraits Des Principales Dames De La Porte Du Grand Turc, *c. 1650.*
In a tall hat heavily veiled.

[3] Blue and black were regarded as the same colour.

34

yellow for Jews, blue for Christians and red for Samaritans. Non-Muslims, men and women, wore the corded girdle *(zunnâr)* and a badge. According to some authorities one of these distinctions was sufficient. Women, besides wearing the appropriate colour, had to wear non-matching shoes: red and black or black and white. Christians were treated with greater severity than Jews and it was not unknown for them to borrow yellow turbans from Jews when feeling ran high against them.

There was no prohibition against non-Muslims wearing a turban provided it conformed to the prescribed colour and did not exceed a certain length. Nevertheless, the turban was the symbol of Mahomed and the distinctive head-dress for non-Muslims was the *kalansuwa*, a hat of Persian origin which went out of fashion among Moslems in the eighth century and when worn by them was usually draped with a scarf to form a turban.

In its later form the *kalansuwa* was tall and coneshaped probably like that worn by Chinese Jews.

In Persia by edict of Abbas I (*c.* 1557–1628) all Jews of the empire were ordered to wear a felt hat like that worn by slaves.

A traveller who visited Persia towards the

34 *TURKEY: Seventeenth century*
DONA EBREA IN CASA. *Drawing*
British Museum Sloane 5255
Tall hat with veil.

35 *TURKEY: 1714*
JUIF. *Engraving*
From De Ferriol
Rubens (ii) 1875
According to the author the distinctive Jewish dress at this time was black clothing and a round violet turban with a checkered border. This is the later version of the Sephardi hat which now has a scarf draped round it. He wears an entari *with girdle under his* caftan.

36 *TURKEY: 1714*
FEMME JUIVE COURTIERE. *Engraving*
From De Ferriol
Rubens (ii) 1877
One of the Jewish women whose business it was to supply goods to the Sultan's harem. She wears a distinctive head-dress which is not worn by any of the Turkish women in this series.

35

36

37

end of the seventeenth century observed that
the Jews wore a hat of a special colour and
also a square patch of cloth on their coats.[4]
According to Benjamin, in the middle of the
nineteenth century the Jews no longer had a
distinctive dress, except that the women were
obliged to wear black veils instead of white
ones when they appeared in public. However at the end of the century Curzon still
found a badge being worn in certain parts of
the country.

Under Ottoman rule Jews were on the
whole favourably treated and in many parts
of the empire developed their own national
costume. The further they were removed
from the seat of central government the
greater were the restrictions, and in the case
of North Africa these were not relaxed
until after the French occupation during the
nineteenth century. Turkey, Syria, Palestine
and the countries of North Africa which had
important Jewish communities are dealt
with separately below.

AUTHORITIES: W. Bacher; S. W. Baron; J. J. Benjamin;
G. N. Curzon; *Encyc. of Islam*; H. Goetz; *Jewish Encyc.*;
R. Levy; I. Lichtenstadter; L. A. Mayer; A. U. Pope;
E. Strauss; A. S. Tritton. *(See Bibliography)*

37 *TURKEY: Smyrna c. 1830*
HABILLEMENT DES JUIFS DE SMYRNE. *Lithograph*
Rubens (ii) 1777
His kaveze *is slightly different to the one worn at Constanti-
nople. He wears a striped* entari *with girdle under a* djubba.

38–39 *TURKEY: c. 1790*
CHACHAN BACHI
FEMME JUIVE. *Drawings. British Museum Add. Ms. 22368
The drawing of the head of the community at Constantinople
was published in* The Costume of Turkey, *1802 [Plate 15].
He wears the traditional Jewish head-dress,* kaveze, *and a
striped* entari *with girdle under a* djubba. *The woman has on
her head the* fotoz *covered by a white sheet worn by Jewish
women at this period.*

40 *TURKEY: Smyrna 1838*
FEMME JUIVE DE SMYRNE. *Lithograph
From E. Fulgenzi,* Collection de Costumes . . . de l'Asie
Mineure, *Smyrna 1838.
Her head is covered with a kerchief and she wears a striped
gown with short fur-trimmed jacket and wooden* chopines.

41 *TURKEY: Constantinople 1846*
JEWISH WOMAN OF PERA. *Lithograph
From Sir David Wilkie's* Sketches in Spain *etc., 1846.
'A Jewess dressed with the Smyrna cap who gave me a sitting;
she was a handsome and elegant person'.
(From the artist's Journal)
She wears a European style dress and her hair is only partly
covered.*

[4] Bacher, 262

38

39

40

41

Turkish Empire

The privileged status which the Jews enjoyed when they first came under Turkish rule was reflected in their dress; such distinctions as existed were retained voluntarily and there were no humiliating restrictions like those suffered in Christian countries. Thus, in 1454, Isaac Zarfati, a Jew of Constantinople, is able to write to the Jews of the Rhineland:

'Is it not better for you to live under Moslems than under Christians? Here every man may dwell at peace under his own vine and his own fig tree. In Christendom on the contrary, ye dare not even venture to clothe your children in red or in blue according to your taste without exposing them to insult and yourself to extortion; and therefore are ye condemned to go about meanly clad in sad-coloured raiment.'[5]

The Jews who fled from Spain in the fifteenth century settled chiefly in Constantinople, Salonica, Adrianople, Brusa, Jerusalem, Safed, Syria and Egypt. Their dress differed from that worn by the native Jews, many of whom were Ashkenazim, and the distinction continued for at least two centuries. Hans Dernschwam, about the middle of the sixteenth century, writes:

'The Jews of Turkey wear clothes according to the language they speak. Usually the garments are long like a *caftan* which is a long tunic tied about the waist over which is a sort of skirt made of cloth of good quality and silk. Just as Turks wear white turbans, the Jews wear yellow. Some foreign Jews still wear the black Italian birettas. Some who pretend to be physicians wear the red pointed elongated birettas.'[6]

George Sandys (1578-1644), who travelled through Turkey at the beginning of the seventeenth century, noted various peculiarities about Jewish costume. At Zycanthus in Greece the Jews wore a blue ribbon on their hats. He was struck by the fact that while in Christendom they were obliged to wear different clothing, in Turkey they did so voluntarily and he described their dress:

'Their undergarments, differing little from the Turks in fashion, are of purple cloth, over that they wear gowns of the same colour with large wide sleeves and clasped beneath the chin without band or collar; on their heads high brimless caps of purple . . . they shave their heads all over . . . their familiar language is Spanish . . . to speak a word or two of their women: the elder mabble (i.e. muffle) their heads in linnen with the knots hanging down behind. Others do wear high caps of plate whereof some I have seen of beaten gold. They wear long quilted waistcoats with breeches underneath; in winter of cloth, in summer of linnen, and over all, when they stir abroad, loose gowns of purple flowing from the shoulders.'[7]

[5] Graetz iv:272. *Jewish Encyclopaedia* xii:280
[6] Quoted by Marcus   [7] Sandys, 7, 114-116

Sumptuary laws existed in Turkey as they did in Europe. In 1554 the rabbis of Salonica passed the following law which was to run for 10 years and was renewed in 1564:

'Women who have reached puberty and especially married women are forbidden to wear in the streets any jewels of gold or silver except for one plain ring on the finger. Jewels may be worn only inside the house.'

Michel Febre, a Capuchin monk who lived for 18 years in Turkey during the middle of the seventeenth century, observed that the Spanish and Portuguese Jews wore a peculiar head-dress 'like a brimless Spanish hat' while the 'native' Jews had coloured turbans and could be distinguished from the Christians only by the colour of their shoes. These were black or violet, the only forbidden colour being green which was reserved for Moslems.[8] De Thevenot, who travelled in the Levant in the seventeenth century, writes:

'The Jews in Turkey dress like the Turks except that they may not wear green, nor a white turban, nor a red jacket. They are usually dressed in violet but they are obliged to wear a violet bonnet *(bonnet)* made in the shape of and the same height as a hat *(chapeau)*, and those who have the means to own a turban wear it round the base of their bonnet. They must also wear socks *(mest)* and violet slippers *(paboudj)*. Jewish and Christian subjects of the Grand Seigneur pay an annual tribute. Those who are not his subjects, in order to prove their exemption wear a hat *(chapeau)* and carry a certificate from a Consul proving their nationality.'[9]

Dandini, another seventeenth century writer, observed that there were at least 500 Jews living at Tripoli in Syria, mostly Spanish or Portuguese, and that they normally wore 'a red bonnet, half a foot high, flat and round'.[10]

The earliest illustrations of Turkish Jews appear in N. de Nicolay's *Les Quatre Premiers Livres Des Navigations . . . Orientales* published at Lyons in 1568. Numerous other editions followed and the plates were pirated for books of costume during the next two centuries. Nicolay's 'Medecin Juif' [Plate 25] who can be identified as Moses Hamon, physician to Sulaiman the Magnificent (1520-66), is bearded and reveals his Sephardi ancestry by wearing 'a high topped cappe' of red scarlet. The 'Marchant Juif' [Plate 29] who, we are told, wears a yellow turban as a mark of distinction is presumably a native Jew. The 'Femme Juifve' of Adrianople [Plate 32] does not appear to be wearing distinctive dress, but has her head 'mabbled' in linen as described by Sandys.

A Jew of Constantinople whose portrait

[8] *Jewish Encyclopaedia* xii:s.v. 'Turkey'
[9] De Thevenot, 264
[10] Dandini, 282

42

appears on an English manuscript dated 1618 [Plate 30] has the high Sephardi hat like that of Moses Hamon. His wife [Plate 31] wears a curious pointed hat to which is attached a long piece of material; she also appears to be wearing false hair, one end of which forms a tail terminating in a tassel. Her long-sleeved dress is worn under a short-sleeved jacket fitting tightly at the waist and trimmed with fur. This garment is European in style and may well have been imported from Spain like the coiffure which is similar to that found in Morocco. George de la Chappelle's 'Femme Juifve' of Constantinople [Plate 33], also of the seventeenth century and, as the artist informs us, taken from life on the spot has a similar pointed hat but her dress is different.

Further evidence of male Sephardi dress in the seventeenth century is supplied by two engravings of Jews from the Holy Land one of which is shown on Plate 50. The other, which has similar costume, is described by Eugene Roger, a French missionary. He makes a sharp distinction between the native Jews of the Orient living in Palestine and those who had originated from Europe, particularly from Spain, and whose tongue was still Spanish. The most intelligent of

42 *TURKEY: Constantinople 1873*
JUIVE DE CONSTANTINOPLE. *Photograph*
From Hamdy-Bey
A yemeni *painted with large flowers with a white fringe is bound round the forehead completely covering the hair. This, particularly the fringe (oya), was worn by all married Jewish women. In other respects there is nothing unusual about the costume: a silk* entari *striped or checked hemmed with gold braid with a belt and a coloured* hyrka *lined and hemmed with white astrakhan. (Hamdy-Bey's description)*

43 *TURKEY: 1862*
JEWISH MARRIAGE. *Lithograph*
From Van Lennep. See p. 48

44 *TURKEY: Salonica 1873*
HAHAM BACHI DE SELANIK. *Photograph*
From Hamdy-Bey
The head of the Salonica community has side locks (peoth). He wears an entari *of striped silk under a* djubba *of fine cloth. The colours are dark and the whole costume is quiet and restrained so as to set a good example. His footwear is the traditional* mest *(socks) and* paboudj *(slippers) in black leather. (Hamdy-Bey's description)*

45

these, he tells us, practised as physicians or farmed the customs and they all dressed alike.

All these engravings are consistent with the descriptions of Jewish costume quoted above, but the traditional *mest* and *paboudj* mentioned by De Thevenot are not heard of again until the nineteenth century when they were noticed by Hamdy-Bey [see Plate 59].

The next series of engravings of Jewish costume appears in an album published in 1714 with text by M. de Ferriol, French ambassador to Turkey. He describes the Jews as being dressed in black and wearing a round violet turban with a checkered border, as shown on Plate 35. This is the earliest illustration of the head-dress described by De Thevenot which is a compromise between the tall brimless hat formerly worn by the Sephardim and the turban of the native Jews. In its typical form, with the two lobes of the turban padded out on each side and twisted so as to leave the base of the hat exposed above the forehead, it remained the characteristic Jewish headgear for men in most parts of the Turkish empire until the end of the nineteenth century. Hamdy-Bey calls it a *kaveze*.

The Jews of Smyrna developed their own traditional dress [Plates 37 & 40] as did those of Salonica [Plates 44 &c.] and it seems that

45 *TURKEY: Smyrna 1873*
HAHAM DE SMYRNE. *Photograph*
From Hamdy-Bey
The leader of the Smyrna community wears a dignified costume in keeping with his office. His bonneto, *a kind of turban, is different from that worn by Moslems but somewhat resembles the turban worn by doctors and divines. He carries a long cane and wears a grey cashmere scarf with fringes round his waist, a long* entari *of striped silk over which is a dark-coloured* binich *with long hanging sleeves,* mest *(socks) and* paboudj *(slippers). (Hamdy-Bey's description)*

46 *TURKEY: c. 1890*
JÜDINNEN AUS DER TÜRKEI. *Engraving*
Their head-dress is the traditional Jewish fotoz *with a white sheet and over their backs they wear a* feradjé *of a special design.*

47 *TURKEY: Salonica 1873*
DAME JUIVE DE SELANIK. *Photograph*
From Hamdy-Bey
The chief characteristic of the costume is the head-dress, a net made of pearls resting on an avlou, *a square of cotton, designed to cover the hair completely. She wears a long* entari *which trails behind; over it, a* fistan *and over all a* djubba *of fine cloth lined with silk and ornamented with fur. Her shoes are European in style. (Hamdy-Bey's description)*

48 *TURKEY: Salonica 1913*
[JEWS IN SABBATH DRESS] *Photograph*
From Mayer

46

47

48

49

throughout Turkey the Jews dressed as they pleased, except that certain colours were prohibited. Lt.-Col. Charles Hamilton Smith (1776–1859), who lived in Turkey in the 1820's and was a careful observer of costume, makes this comment:

'Christians and Jews are not allowed to wear brilliant colours. They are obliged to choose such as are dull even in painting the outside of their houses. In Egypt, however, little thought is given this order and excepting green all colours may be worn. With the Turks green is a sacred colour and is only worn by themselves though they also have all other colours. Europeans are indulged with permission to have yellow slippers but Oriental Christians and Jews are confined to red, blue or black.'[11]

The richness and variety of Jewish costume in different parts of the Turkish empire may be judged by the accompanying illustrations.

Women in particular developed the most elaborate wardrobes which usually had special characteristics to distinguish them from Moslem dress.

The picture of a Jewish wedding [Plate 43], published in 1862, was sketched by an American missionary, the Rev. Henry J. Van Lennep, who attended the ceremony after having had the bride's dress sent to his lodgings so that he could faithfully represent in colours the minutest details; in addition to

49 *TURKEY: Brusa 1873*
JUIF ET JUIVES DE BROUSSE. *Photograph*
From Hamdy-Bey
The man's head-dress, called kaveze, *consists of a high crown of cardboard covered with black material around which is rolled a piece of light-colour cotton. The only other distinctive feature of his dress is the lining of his* djubba *which is white on top and black at the bottom. Moslems and Christians wear a lining all of one colour.*
The women, like all the Jewish women of the East, have different dress for the house and the street. The woman on the left is dressed in the peculiar fotoz *in which they bury their hair so that it cannot be seen after they are married. She wears an* entari, *open in front, of rich flowered silk with a scarf tied round the waist, a* hyrka *without sleeves, lined and edged with fur and* paboudj *(slippers) of yellow morocco.*
The woman on the right, dressed for the street, wears a fotoz *covered with a* yachmak *to which are attached jewels which hang down in front of her nose and cheeks. The* feradjé *which is of a special shape, distinguishes the Jewish from the Moslem women. It is a piece of silk worn like a scarf from above the breast and down the back. (Hamdy-Bey's description)*

50 *PALESTINE: Seventeenth century*
JUIF DE LA TERRE SAINTE. *Etching*
From H. Bonnart, Recueil d'estampes de Costumes du XVIIe Siècle, *Paris c. 1690. Jewish Theological Seminary. The typical Sephardi costume in Turkey: tall hat, fur-trimmed* pelisse, entari *and girdle.*

[11] Victoria & Albert Museum, Print Room. Ms. D. 374. 1890. 93 B9.

51

this he supplies the following description:

'The Bridegroom was 20 and the Bride 12. They stood up in their Bridal garments under a tent-like structure supported by poles and made of cloths belonging to the Bride's dowry, erected in the largest apartment in her parent's house. The remainder of the dowry besides what she wore, was contained in two green chests which stood behind them and were used as seats by the pair. The Bride's pasteboard horn was the same as the Armenian bride with this difference, that no veil was thrown over it in the present case. Natural and artificial flowers and sprigs of wormwood adorned her head like a crown. Her veil was of gauze and perfectly transparent and her eyes remained closed during the whole ceremony. Two tall candlesticks stood before them on which tallow candles burned all the while. . . . The mothers of the parties stood by them closely veiled during the ceremony soon after the conclusion of which the bride's peculiar ornaments were removed from her and she was allowed freely to mingle with the company.'

Another reliable eye-witness was an Englishwoman, Lucy M. J. Garnett, who, in 1891, published a study of the women of Turkey in which she gives this description of the costume of the Jewish women:

'The ancient costumes which all the native Jews continue to wear are, on the whole, exceedingly picturesque and curious. They vary slightly according to locality, the head-dress at Smyrna being different in style and material from that worn at Salonica where the costume is particularly ornate. Here the married women put away

51 *PALESTINE: Jerusalem c. 1830*
H. Z. SNEERSOHN OF JERUSALEM. *Wood engraving*
Mocatta Library
He was otherwise known as Dob Bär B. Shneor Zalman Ladier (c. 1770–1834) head of a Russian Hasidic sect known as Habad founded by his father.
He wears a fez *and a striped* entari *with girdle under a* djubba.

52 *PALESTINE: 1840*
A JEW DRAGOMAN OF THE BRITISH CONSUL TEACHING CHILDREN. *Drawing by David Wilkie inscribed 'A Jew Dragoman at Jerusalem, 1840'. National Gallery of Scotland.*
He wears a fez *and a fur-trimmed* djubba.

53 *PALESTINE: Jerusalem c. 1850*
DAVID, SON OF RABBI SAMUEL MAJHA 2ND CHIEF RABBI OF JERUSALEM. *Lithograph*
Jewish Theological Seminary
He wears the traditional kaveze *with a striped* entari *under a* djubba.

54 *PALESTINE: Jerusalem 1842*
JEWISH FAMILY ON MOUNT ZION. *Engraving*
From Bartlett. See p. 52

52

53

54

55

their back hair in a rectangular bag of silk or stuff about 12 inches in length and 3 to 4 in width, the extremity being ornamented with embroidery and terminated by a fringe frequently of seed pearls. This bag is attached to a kind of cap which covers the top of the head, round which fine muslin handkerchiefs are twisted, one of them passing under the chin, strings of seed pearls and gold coins being added for full dress. The costume consists chiefly of 2 or 3 gowns, or rather long tight jackets, open from the hip downwards, worn one over the other, and full Turkish trousers. None of these garments meet at the throat but leave the chest bare, or at most only partially covered by the gauze vests worn by the wealthy, or the coarse cotton gown which forms the under-garment of the poor. The materials vary from printed cotton to the richest brocaded silk damask, but the designs are always similar—namely wide contrasting stripes with flower patterns stamped over them. For outdoor wear, a long pelisse of dark red cloth, lined and trimmed with fur is added and over the head a fine white Turkish towel, with fringed ends, which does not, however, conceal the face. Handsome gold bracelets and a necklace of pearls complete the costume. Pearls are indeed a passion with Salonica Jewesses who, whatever their rank, spend all the money at their command in these ornaments for their heads and necks.

'The costume of the Jewish women of Constantinople differs chiefly from that of Salonica in the substitution for outdoor wear of a short loose jacket, lined and faced with lambskin, swansdown or squirrel for the long red pelisse. The coiffure is also much more simple being merely a *yemeni*, or large square kerchief of coloured

55 *PALESTINE: Jerusalem 1863*
JEWS AT THE WAILING WALL, JERUSALEM. *Wood Engraving*
From Benjamin
A variety of Western, Polish and Oriental costumes.

56 *PALESTINE: Samaritans 1854*
COSTUME AND LIKENESS OF THE PRESENT SAMARITAN PRIEST, RABBI AMRAM AND HIS FAMILY AT NABLOUS. *Lithograph*
From Jerusalem and the Holy Land . . . from drawings taken on the spot by Mrs Ewald, *London, 1854.*
Rubens (ii) 1699
One man wears a fez, the other a turban. The woman has a head scarf and wears trousers.

57 *PALESTINE: 1840*
HEBREW WOMAN AND CHILD. *Lithograph by David Wilkie*
From his Sketches in Turkey, Syria and Egypt, *1843.*
Rubens (ii) 1644
The artist comments: 'In their girlhood the Jewish women generally take great pride in the adornment of their hair; but from the time of their marriage it is commonly hidden and for its better concealment a second handkerchief is attached to the turban behind which it descends very low and covers the whole more effectually than the simpler head-dress.'

56

57

58

muslin painted with large flowers and bordered, like the outer gown, with white *oya* lace. This lace border, though rather expensive—or perhaps for that reason—is indispensable. One side of the kerchief is brought low over the forehead, completely concealing the hair, and two of the corners fall over the shoulders behind. This head-dress, however, has only been adopted since the interdiction of the preposterous *chalebi* formerly worn by the Jewesses of the Turkish capital. It consisted of a large ball of cotton wool, or linen rags, tightly compressed, which was placed on the crown of the head and held there by one person while another wound round it, in complicated folds, a shawl or scarf, until it attained monstrous proportions and completely covered the head of the wearer, whom it not only frightfully disfigured but at the same time exposed to the derisive remarks of both Moslems and Christians. (At the request of the Vizier the *chalebi* was prohibited by the Chief Rabbi, to the great indignation of the women).

'The coiffure of the Jewish women of Aleppo is a high dome-shaped cap, made of silk striped in different colours and worn low on the forehead. From under it depends a quantity of false hair, either plaited in tresses or hanging loose over the shoulders. The *fotoz* affected by the Israelite ladies of Broussa, like that formerly worn in the capital, is an enormous cushion of parti-coloured stuffs covered with jewels and strings of pearls some of which hang in festoons over the cheeks. A veil of white muslin is worn over this out of doors and the remainder of the dress is concealed by a *feradjé* or cloak differing in colour and also in shape from that worn by Moslem women.'[12]

Bartlett devotes a considerable amount of space to the family seen in Plate 54, the head of which he describes as the wealthiest Jew of Jerusalem, although not a native of the city. He continues:

'We found him seated on the low divan fondling his youngest child and on our expressing a wish to draw the costume of the female members of his family he commanded their attendance.... Their costume (as represented in the illustration) was chastely elegant.

'The prominent figure in the sketch is the married daughter, whose little husband, a boy of fourteen or fifteen, as he seemed, wanted nearly a head of the stature of his wife, but was already chargeable with the onerous duties of a father. An oval head-dress of peculiar shape, from which is slung a long veil of embroidered muslin, shown as hanging, in the sketch, from the back of another figure, admirably sets off the brow and eyes; the neck is ornamented with bracelets, and the bosom with a profusion of gold coins, partly concealed by folds of muslin; a graceful robe of striped silk, with long open sleeves, half-laced under the bosom, invests the whole person, over which is worn a jacket of green silk with short sleeves, leaving the white arm and braceleted hand at liberty. The elder person on the sofa is the mother, whose dress was more grave, her turban less oval, and of blue shawl, and the breast covered, entirely to the neck, with a kind of ornamented gold tissue, above which is seen a jacket of fur: she was engaged in knitting, while her younger daughter bent over her in conversation: her dress is similar to that of her sister, but

[12] Garnett, 13 ff.

59

58 *PALESTINE: 1866*

SPANISH JEWESSES WEARING THE MOON-SHAPED TURBAN.
Engraving. From Finn. See p. 54
They are in the typical head-dress (fotoz) *worn by Jewish women.*

59 *PALESTINE: Jerusalem 1873*

JUIF DE JERUSALEM, JUIVE DE JERUSALEM. *Photograph*
From Hamdy-Bey
The man has a dignified appearance.
His head-dress is a black kaveze *widening out at the top to form a polygon, surrounded by a turban of white muslin ribbed and divided in two lobes stretched to the right and left of his head and padded out. The material is folded so as to leave the base of the hat in front and behind uncovered. Round his neck he wears a cashmere scarf with a border of* palmettes *arranged with great neatness and his* djubba *of white cashmere is worn with the same precision over a long* entari *of white silk with pink stripes. Round his waist he wears a rich scarf of cashmere artistically tied which trails to the ground covering his footwear which are* mest *(socks) and* paboudj *(slippers) of black morocco.*
The woman's fistan *is of dark green decorated with gold embroidery. Its long open sleeves are brought through the narrow sleeves of the* salta *which is of white cashmere. Her head-dress, the* fotoz, *is decorated with a large number of* yemeni, *handkerchiefs painted with flowers, arranged one on top of the other in the shape of a melon. To the borders are attached sequins and gold pins which hang over the nose and cheeks producing a strange effect. A* bach eurtussu *of white muslin fixed to the top of the* fotoz *frames the face, crosses under the chin and hangs over the arms and back. The footwear consists of* mest *(socks) and* paboudj *(slippers) of black morocco. (Hamdy-Bey's description)*

60

with no gold coins or tight muslin folds; and instead of large earrings, the vermilion blossom of the pomegranate formed an exquisite pendant, reflecting its glow upon the dazzling whiteness of her skin.

'We were surprised at the fairness and delicacy of their complexions, and the vivacity of their manner. Unlike the wives of oriental Christians, who respectfully attend at a distance till invited to approach, these pretty Jewesses seemed on a perfect footing of equality, and chatted and laughed without intermission.'[13]

Mrs Finn makes several observations about Jewish costume in Jerusalem between 1846 and 1863 when her husband, James Finn, was British Consul. The Jewish women of Jerusalem wore a white sheet, but not a coloured handkerchief over the face like the Moslem and Christian women. The Oriental rabbis she met wore full trousers of crimson cloth, a vest of light Damascus silk and a cloth robe with ample gray turban most carefully folded. Mrs Finn also visited the Jewish family on Mount Zion mentioned by Bartlett and gives this description:

'A servant conducted us into an upper room, which I at once recognized as the room in the frontispiece of "Bartlett's Walks". The lady of the house came forward and greeted us with much cordiality. She was small, slight, and very fair in complexion, and did not look more than forty. Her dress was rich: a sky-blue jacket, and white silk skirt embroidered with silver, just

60 *PALESTINE: Jerusalem 1854*
COSTUME AND LIKENESS OF A NATIVE JEW AND JEWESS OF JERUSALEM. *Lithograph*
From Jerusalem and the Holy Land . . . from drawings taken on the spot by Mrs Ewald, *London, 1854*
Both in traditional Jewish dress; the man wearing kaveze, *striped* entari *with girdle under a* djubba; *the woman in characteristic head-dress* (fotoz).

61 *MESOPOTAMIA: Baghdad 1949*
HAHAMIM AND RABBIS OF BAGHDAD. *Photograph*
From D. S. Sassoon, A History of the Jews in Baghdad, *Letchworth 1949.*
All wear girdles and native dress.

[13] Bartlett, 192–3

61

below which peeped full trousers of pale yellow silk and little green Morocco slippers. The head-dress was a turban, projecting forwards in a halfmoon shape, and down the back hung a white muslin veil spangled with gold.

'Two pretty daughters, dressed in the same manner as their mother, stood ready to make their salaam, as soon as she had done greeting her guests. They led us to the divan, and then repeated the salaams. Mr Andersen spoke with them in Spanish, and Mary in Arabic.

'Meanwhile I observed the gold necklaces and bracelets which the ladies wore. The necklaces were a sort of fringe, composed of separate little pointed ornaments of gold, something like sharks' teeth. The bracelets were much hand-somer, and composed of a multitude of beauti-fully-wrought flexible chains. The long clasps were thickly set with diamonds.

'Small chains of gold and festoons of pearls were attached to the turban, and one wore a large emerald depending on her forehead.

'The mother had a variety of diamond ornaments set on her turban, and they all wore fresh flowers intermingled with the jewellery. Two pretty little boys sat shyly at the lower end of the divan. Their red caps were ornamented with gold coins; but, like all other children that we had seen, they were spoiled in appearance by the old-fashioned, clumsy look of their clothes; jackets and full trousers, such as men wore, sat awkwardly upon these little fellows . . .'[14]

Mrs Finn's brother, Walter, made a sketch of the two daughters called 'Spanish Jewesses wearing the moon-shaped Turban' [Plate 58].

[14] Finn, 190–1

The same type of turban is seen in Plate 46.

The late Israel Abrahams, in a letter to his wife dated 10 April 1898 from Jerusalem, describes the Jewish promenade on the Jaffa road on a Saturday evening. He writes:

'The people pass and repass in all costumes—(by the way again, many here also wear European dress all the week, but revert to Oriental costume on Sabbaths and Festivals). There is nothing in the world, I should think, quite like the Jerusalem costumes. There is more variety, less brilliancy than in Cairo. It is an idealized East End of London. The people bring all the costumes of the world here, then borrow from each other, and thus in the end I have no doubt that a Jerusalem type of costume will evolve itself. Each man plays several parts. I have just given you one instance. Now I meet the same people on the same day at different houses (I pay lots of visits) and find them differently dressed. Especially does this apply to the head-dress. A man wears different styles to suit his hosts. This is not a common thing, but it occurs often enough to excite one's notice.'[15]

An English traveller who visited Bokhara at the beginning of the nineteenth century found the Jews wearing distinctive dress and a conical cap. The women, who were remark-ably handsome, wore their hair in ringlets covering their cheeks and neck.[16] When Adler was in Bokhara in 1896 the Jews were still wearing a Badge and until the Soviet

[15] Quoted by kind permission of Dr Phyllis Abrahams
[16] Burnes ii, 235

62

government was established they were required to wear a special type of fur cap instead of a turban and to tie a rope round their waist. They shaved their heads but wore side locks *(peoth)*[17] [see Plate 62]. After the Russian occupation in 1868 a number of Bokharan Jews settled in Samarcand which had previously been barred to them. When Count Pahlen visited that province in 1908 he found the local Jews dressed in brightly coloured caftans with a silken cord in lieu of the usual ceremonial sash, which Jews were not allowed to wear. The ornate Bokharan dress seen in Israel today [Plate 70] was probably adopted in fairly recent times.

Adler, who visited the Caucasus at the end of the nineteenth century, found the Jews wearing a high black (or occasionally white) astrakhan fez, but otherwise in national costume with bandoliers [see Plate 69]. The Jews of Afghanistan still wear a fur hat as a mark of distinction.[18]

At the beginning of the twentieth century the Jews of Aden had *peoth* and wore *arba kanphoth*. Their *tallith*, which was called *mandil* (Arabic = kerchief or shawl), had green silk corners. The women wore trousers and a wig called *masr* and they were veiled like the Moslem women. The more recent

62 *RUSSIAN TURKESTAN: Samarcand c. 1870*
JEWS OF SAMARCAND. *Wood engraving*
Mocatta Library
A feature of their dress appears to be the striped material. The men have side locks (peoth).

63 *PALESTINE: Jerusalem c. 1870*
JÜDEN AUS JERUSALEM. *Engraving*
They are in Polish Jewish costume

64 *SYRIA: 1590*
HEBREA. *Wood engraving*
From Vecellio, Abiti Antici, *Venice 1590. According to the author the Jewish women wore a tall coiffure covered by a silk veil with a silk band underneath cunningly arranged to cover the hair. The skirt is short and is of silk with bands round the hem.*

65 *RUSSIAN TURKESTAN: Samarcand c. 1900*
[JEWESS OF SAMARCAND] *Photograph*
From Jewish Encyclopædia *x:668.*

[17] *Jewish Encyclopaedia* iii, 294
[18] See *Jewish Chronicle* 1 September 1961

64

63

65

66

costume of a bride of the Habani tribe [Plate 76] has other features and in the Yemen Jewish women possessed an even more elaborate wardrobe with many special characteristics[19] [Plate 71].

A great variety of Jewish costume from Turkestan, Kurdistan, Yemen and Aden is to be seen now in museums at Haifa, Tel-Aviv and Jerusalem.

AUTHORITIES: E. N. Adler; S. W. Baron; W. H. Bartlett; A. Burnes; A. Danon; L. M. J. Garnett; W. Macmichael; J. R. Marcus; Museum of Ethnography & Folklore, Tel-Aviv.   Description of costume exhibits; K. K. Pahlen; D. S. Sassoon.   *(See Bibliography)*

Egypt

At the end of the fifteenth century the distinctive dress of the Jews of Cairo was a yellow turban while Christians and Moslems wore blue and white turbans respectively.[20] Two centuries later, according to De Bruyn, the Jews had to wear a turban of blue stripes and violet coloured clothing. The women wore long black hats with a white or brown kerchief striped with gold and silver [Plate 73].

When Lane was in Egypt between 1825 and 1849 there was very little distinction in dress between Jews and Moslems but Jews and Christians wore turbans of the same colour. The women veiled themselves and in

66 *BOSNIA: Nineteenth century*
Photograph
Jewish Historical Museum, Belgrade
The traditional ceremonial dress of the Sephardi women of Sarajevo. The hat was known as tocado de Belogrado.

[19] See A. Lancet 'Costumes de Mariage des Juifs de San'a et leurs survivances en Israël' in *Actes due VIe Congrès International . . .* Paris 1960 ii:i.
[20] Von Harff, 113

67

68

67 *RUSSIAN TURKESTAN: Bokhara 1915*
JEWESS FROM BOKHARA. *Etching. By E. M. Lilien*
Lilien Catalogue No. 117.

68 *SYRIA: Aleppo 1873*
DAME JUIVE D'HALEP. *Photograph*
From Hamdy-Bey
*The head-dress is peculiar to Aleppo. The author remarks that
in many parts of the Orient when Jewish women cut off their
hair after marriage, it was the practice to ornament their
head-dress with cock's feathers or white fringes. Only in
Aleppo, apparently, did they wear a wig. This women wears a
kind of mitre of striped silk to which is attached a trimming
of false hair and long tresses. The long* entari *of silk with
wide red and yellow stripes has no sleeves. She also wears a*
chalwar *which cannot be seen, a* mintan *of the same material
as the* entari *with excessively long sleeves fitting tightly
round the arms and opening out past the hands, a* hyrka *of
light colour closed up to the neck, the tight sleeves of which
finish above the elbows. A scarf of silk and cotton is worn
round the waist. The skirt of the* entari *is gathered in little
pleats round the hips and falls stiffly covering the shoes which
are either* tchédik *(soft boots) or yellow* paboudj *(slippers).*
(Hamdy-Bey's description)

69

69 *RUSSIA : Caucasus c. 1930*
JEW OF THE CAUCASUS. *Photograph*
From Jüdisches Lexikon *III, 637*
In typical fur hat and carrying bandolier as described by Adler.

70 *RUSSIAN TURKESTAN : Bokhara twentieth century*
[WEDDING] *Models*
Museum of Ethnography and Folklore, Tel-Aviv
*The children on the left are performing a traditional dance.
They are dressed in smocks called* kamzoli frangi masko *and
the boy also wears a long shirt, the* frangi. *Behind them is the
bridegroom in a coat ornately embroidered in gold with a star
design. On his head he wears a brocade band, the* sala kundal.
His cap, the kalpak kundal, *is exhibited on the wall over
the bride's head. She is being 'made up' by her mother who
wears a dress covered with sequins called* kurti plaktché.
Both wear a cap, the topi arktchin. *Over it the bride has a veil
of tulle spangled with sequins, the* plaktché, *to which is
attached a large gold ornament set with gems, the* parchona.
*Her gown is of brocade shot with gold thread and her hair is in
many plaits threaded singly through the meshes of a special net
knotted from black thread and adorned with gilt globes. A
member of the bridegroom's family is handing the bride the*
sivlonoth, *the presents from the bridegroom.*

public dressed like the Egyptian women.

Benjamin, who visited Egypt in the course of his travels between 1846 and 1855, gives this description of Jewish costume:

'The dress of the Egyptian Jews is like that worn by the Jews in Turkey. Many wear white turbans, and they often dress with great splendour. The women are also attired like those of Turkey; their head-dress alone differs from that of the Turkish Jewesses, for they wear a red fez, the tassel of which consists of long single silken threads, hanging down to the feet. At the end of each thread is attached a silver or some other coin, whereby this head-dress is made very heavy. I once had such a fez in my hand, and I should reckon its weight to have been about ten pounds. The long tassels with the coins attached to them cause quite a ringing sound when the women appear in the street.'[21]

Tripoli

According to Lyon, who visited Tripoli between 1818 and 1820, the Jews wore blue turbans and black shoes. The women dressed like the Moslem women except that they were allowed only black or yellow shoes and when they went out they left both eyes uncovered instead of only one.

A rather different account is given by Benjamin:

'Many dress in the same fashion as in Tunis, others in the fashion of Algiers, and many others

[21] Benjamin, 283

70

71 *YEMEN: Sa'ana twentieth century*
[JEWISH WEDDING] *Models*
Museum of Ethnography and Folklore, Tel-Aviv
The bride wears a complete set of bridal ornaments known as
teshbuch-lulu *arranged in a formal pattern. The bridal*
crown is different from that worn by Moslem women. Other
features of her dress are the shmeelat *(bracelets) and the*
mekhukhavim *(leggings). The bridegroom, dressed in a*
caftan, *wears on his breast a silver circle, the* tok, *from which*
is suspended a triangular-shaped bag, the chraté.

72 *PERSIA: c. 1850*
A PERSIAN AN ISRAELITE. *Drawing*
In turban and caftan *with girdle.*

71

72

F

73

wear a peculiar costume consisting of a long garment reaching to the knees, a short burnos, white trowsers reaching to the knees, and red shoes. The women wear for head-dress a red fez wound round with a silk kerchief, and beautifully ornamented in different ways. To this is added a long garment, and a wide shawl hanging from the head, thrown gracefully round the upper part of the body. They wear slippers but no stockings, their hands and feet are covered with gold and silver rings, the nails painted red and the eyebrows black.'[22]

Tunisia

The Jewish community goes back to Roman times and the normal restrictions on dress would have applied from the beginning of Arab rule. By the sixteenth century the special dress worn by men, like that of Jews in other parts of North Africa under Moslem rule, was a blue collarless tunic with loose sleeves, wide linen drawers, black slippers and a black skull cap. The dress of Jewish women has attracted little comment from travellers presumably as it had no special features; it is like that worn in Algeria [Plate 74].

Benjamin, visiting the country on his travels (1846–55), gives this description of the costume of the Jews in Tunis:

'The men wear wide cloth trowsers, stockings, and shoes, an embroidered vest, and over this a

73 *EGYPT: 1698*
FEMME JUIVE. *Engraving*
From C. de Bruyn, Reizen, *Delft, 1698*
She wears a very long black hat covered with a white or brown kerchief striped with gold and silver. The clothes of the Jewish women were usually of striped silk.

74 *TUNIS: c. 1840*
JUIFS TUNISIENS. *Wood engraving*
Jewish Theological Seminary
The man wears a turban and native costume; the women in cârmas, ghlîlas *and* djubbas *like the Algerian Jewesses.*

75 *RHODES: 1873*
JUIF DE RHÔDES; JUIVE DE RHÔDES. *Photograph*
From Hamdy-Bey
The man is dressed very simply. His head-dress is a fez encircled by a yemeni *(painted handkerchief). He wears a long* entari *of silk or cotton, a* djubba *of cloth and black shoes. The woman is dressed even more simply; a good* entari *of cotton, a* chalwar *and over all an excellent* djubba *of silk or fine cloth through which pass the sleeves of the* entari. *Her head-dress is a cotton bonnet* (takke) *under two* yemeni *kerchiefs designed to conceal the hair which no good Jewish woman wears uncovered from the day of her marriage. Her shoes are black* paboudj *(slippers). (Hamdy-Bey's description)*

76 *ADEN: Hadramauth twentieth century*
[BRIDE OF THE HABANI TRIBE] *Model*
Museum of Ethnography and Folklore, Tel-Aviv
Habani female dress does not include the trousers worn by Yemenite women and the bride's costume is completely different. Her hair is braided into heavy plaits and is not covered but a small triangular portion of her head above the temple is shaved.

[22] Benjamin, 287–8

74

75

76

burnos. They shave their heads; the unmarried men wear a small black cap, and the married ones a turban with a black fez. The women wear a folded garment and wide trowsers of silk or satin, which are quite tight from the knee, and ornamented with rich embroideries of gold and silver. Over all this they put on a kind of silk tunic, without sleeves, reaching as far as the knee, composed generally of two different coloured kinds of stuff. They cover their head with a fez, round which is wound a silk kerchief, with the ends hanging down. They likewise wear stockings and shoes. Upon their trowsers, in particular, great extravagance is lavished; and I was told that they often cost the rich from 400 to 500 reals. The married women wear round their waist a kind of girdle. In the street they wrap themselves in a wide silk or fine woollen shawl; but leave their face uncovered, and hold up their garments as high as the knee, in order to display the embroidery on their trowsers. They are generally very beautiful, rather stout, and in their beauty resemble their sisters in Baghdad; except that the women in that town are more noble looking and graceful, while the ladies of Tunis are more corpulent. The Baghdad ladies are very industrious, while it is quite the contrary with those in Tunis. In Tunis as well as in Baghdad the girls marry from the age of thirteen and upwards.'[23]

Hesse-Warteg, writing in 1882, states that the Jews of Tunis had not become emancipated as rapidly as those of Algeria and could still be distinguished at once by their appearance and dress which he describes thus.

'Tall and strongly-built, with fine, noble features and long beards, they show still more to advantage in their peculiar, picturesque costumes. They are not bound to wear a certain dress, as formerly, but they seem desirous of their hereditary appearance. They have only changed their head-dress. Formerly they were forbidden to wear the red fez or sheshia of the Arab, but wore the prescribed black turban wound round a white fez—a kind of nightcap. They have now adopted the red fez, but keep to the black turban, while the younger generation has given up the turban altogether. They are allowed to wear the white turban of the Arabs, but they never make use of this permission. Their short jackets are of a light colour, richly embroidered with gold and open in front; and while the old orthodox Jews still keep to the black trousers, with many folds tied below the knee, the younger generation has adopted light-coloured ones. They all wear snow-white stockings; and the yellow or red leather slippers of the Arabs have been discarded by the Jewish swell in favour of the patent leather shoes imported from Europe, but which he treads down, so that his heel projects one or two inches beyond the shoe. A broad shawl, generally richly embroidered, is thrown round the loins, and while in winter their costume is completed by a long circular cloak of light-blue colour, they replace this in summer by a fine cloak of spotless whiteness, called the R'fara.

'Neither they nor the Arabs carry arms; and they are scarcely necessary in Tunis, which is safer than European towns. Stately as a Jew's appearance is, and tasteful as is his dress, it is only so as long as he keeps his fez on his head. Like the Arabs, they are in the habit of shaving their heads,

[23] Benjamin, 302

only leaving a small tuft of hair on the top which has a most ludicrous effect. . . .

'The costume of the Jewesses is just as ugly as the dress of the Jews has been shown to be picturesque and beautiful. It is scarcely possible to imagine a toilet more tasteless and odd. Seen from a distance, Jewesses resemble ballet-girls, of whose body the upper part seems wrapped in a sack down to the hips. The stranger who meets such a figure for the first time fancies he sees a woman who has forgotten to dress herself, and is rather perplexed. The costume of a Jewess, whether a child or an old woman, consists of very few articles. Over the nether garment, made of white linen, they wear a small, gold-embroidered velvet jacket, a pair of white, very tight pantaloons, which reach to the ankle, and differ in nothing from the tights of ballet-girls. Short white socks cover, as a rule, their small feet, of which the points are covered by tiny, black kid slippers, scarcely protecting half the foot; or they wear high wooden sandals. Over the upper part of the body a baggy chemise falls down to the hips, made of red, yellow, or light-green silk, and their head is covered by the velvet 'kufia' embroidered in gold and shaped like a sugar-loaf, and is tied by a red or yellow silk ribbon. On their arms and necks they wear heavy gold chains and bracelets, and face and hands are uncovered.'[24]

The same writer describes the costume of a Jewish bride as being of such splendour that it defied description. Her face was covered with a gold-embroidered veil and she wore a gold-brocaded upper garment, velvet pantaloons covered with gold braid, red silk stockings and gold-embroidered slippers. Her fingers were entirely covered with diamonds and dyed down to the second joint with henna.

AUTHORITIES: J. J. Benjamin; De Hesse-Warteg; *Jewish Encyc.* *(See Bibliography)*

Algeria

Jewish settlements in Algeria go back to the Roman era and there has been an important community there since medieval times. Under the Arabs the Jews suffered the same restrictions as they did in other parts of the Moslem Empire. In 1391 many Jewish refugees from Castile, Aragon, Andalusia and the Balearic Islands fled to Algeria. The new-comers were known as 'wearers of Birettas' while the native Algerian Jews were called 'wearers of turbans'.

Native Algerian dress, which Jewish women gradually adopted, owed most of its attraction to Andalusian or Turkish influences.

The earliest description of the Jews is given by Diego De Haedo in a book published at Valladolid in Spain in 1612. He divides the Jews of Algiers into three categories: descendants of Spanish refugees; those from Majorca, France and Italy; and the indigenous Jews of Africa. All carried on a trade of some kind, particularly tailoring and coral

[24] De Hesse-Warteg 117–18, 129

77

working; they were the only ones who coined money, the entire mint being in their hands, and most of the silversmiths were Jews. They traded with Tripoli, Gelves, Tunis, Bone, Constantine, Oran, Tlemcen, Tetuan, Fez, Marrakesh and Constantinople.

The Spanish Jews wore a round cap of Toledo needlework, the Jews from Majorca, France and Italy a black wool garment with half sleeves and a hood; those coming from Constantinople and Turkey wore turbans of choice materials but yellow in colour, and some had top-boots which had to be black. The native Jews wore a red cap around which was wrapped a *toca* (headcloth) of white canvas material. This was like the head-dress of the local Moors and as a distinction the Jews had to leave the forelock uncovered hanging down the centre of the forehead. In other respects all the Jews dressed alike in wide breeches, a shirt, and a long black coat over which was worn an *albornoz* (burnous), usually black but sometimes white. No Jews were allowed to wear proper shoes but were restricted to slippers.

Most of the Jewish women also wore slippers which were always black in colour. When they went out they covered their faces with a delicate white veil secured by a knot

77 *TUNIS: 1850*
RABBI ABRAHAM BELAIS. *Lithograph*
Rubens (i) 316
The Rabbi, who was born in Tunis, retained his native costume after settling in London.

78 *ALGERIA: c. 1796*
EIN ALLGIERISCHER JÜD. *Etching*
From A. M. Wolffgang, Costumes Algériens *c. 1796*
Jewish Theological Seminary
He is bearded and wears head scarf, belted tunic, shirt with voluminous sleeves, burnous, trousers and mules with heels.

79 *TUNIS: c. 1900*
[JEWISH MERCHANT OF THE BAZAAR AND HIS WIFE]
Photograph
The man's dark blue or black turban and blue cloak distinguish him as a Jew. The woman wears typical white pantaloons, white socks and the pointed velvet hat (kufia) embroidered in gold and tied by a red or yellow silk ribbon.

80-81 *ALGERIA: 1835*
JEUNE FEMME JUIVE. *Drawings*
Bibliothèque Nationale.
She wears a djubba *of prune-coloured velvet through the arm-holes of which are brought the sleeves of the* ghlila *and the blouse. Her head-dress is the* çarma. *The back view shows how the sleeves are joined together.*

78

79

80

81

82

at the back of the head leaving the eyes and forehead visible. They also wore a cloak called an *alhuyke* made of very fine white wool or woven silk and wool. There was little to distinguish their costume from that of the Moorish women.

Jewish brides did not paint their arms black as did the Moorish women but used much colour and white cosmetics and adorned themselves with bracelets, rings gold earrings and *aljofar* (a misshapen pearl). The wedding day was a day of fête set aside for music and dancing. The courtyard of the house where the ceremony was held was decorated with silk and the bride sat on a dais like a May Queen. Anyone, Moors and Christians included, could enter and watch.

The Chevalier d'Arvieux, in an account of his travels in Algeria in 1660 published in Paris in 1735, describes a visit to a Jewish wedding. He found nothing unusual about the costume of the Jewish women except that when they went out they were so completely covered from head to toe that only their eyes were visible.

The most striking feature of Algerian Jewish married women's costume during the nineteenth century on gala occasions was the long cone-shaped head-dress on a metal

82 *ALGERIA: 1842*
DEMOISELLE JUIVE D'ALGER. *Coloured lithograph*
Rubens (ii) 1709[e]
She wears a blue and gold djubba *over a blue* ghlîla *the short sleeves of which are tied behind her back. On her head is a* mharma.

83. *ALGERIA: 1833*
JUIVE D'ALGER
Etching by E. Delacroix
Delacroix noted in his journal that he made a drawing of the Jewess, Dititia, in Algerian costume. Her dress, in fact, with its wrap-over skirt embroidered on one corner is more like the ceremonial dress of the Moroccan Jewesses but her head-dress is native Algerian.

84

frame known as the *çârma*, which is similar to the *tantoura* worn by Druse women and the fifteenth-century European *hennin*. It is not known in Algeria before the eighteenth century and its use by Jewish women was first observed by Abraham Salamé, an Egyptian interpreter, who visited the country in 1816. At that period only Turkish or Moorish women were allowed to have *çârmas* made of silver or gold, the Jewish women being restricted to brass, except the wife of Jacob Bacri, banker to the Dey, who wore one of gold. They went out of fashion among Moslems round about 1890.

The normal dress for Jewish women by the middle of the nineteenth century was the native *ghlîla* and *djubba*. The former was a décolletée vest reaching the knees with short sleeves brought through the armholes of the *djubba*, which was an ankle-length gown.

The following description of the Jews was given by an English traveller in 1835:

'The Jews of Barbary shave the head close and allow the beard to grow. They are not permitted to use the turban but wear a small black woollen cap, which merely covers the back of the head, leaving the forehead and temples bare. The shirt is made with very wide sleeves, which hang loose as far as the elbows; over this is a vest of dark cloth, which fastens tight round the neck,

84 *ALGERIA: c. 1840*
JUIF. *Lithograph*
He wears European style shirt with collar and cravat with two jackets of local style: the bed'iya *and the* ghlîla, *the latter with sleeves and edged with buttons. He has stockings and* cobbât *without heels. A* burnous *is slung over his shoulder. The tassel hanging from the turban is a Jewish characteristic.*

85 *ALGERIA: 1835*
FESTIN JUIF. *Lithograph*
From Voyage Pittoresque dans la Regence d'Alger, *Paris 1835*
Rubens (ii) 1708
Feast to celebrate a circumcision with the women all in their ceremonial dresses and çârmas; *the men in turbans.*

86 *ALGERIA: 1842*
JUIF D'ALGER. *Coloured lithograph*
Rubens (ii) 1710
Black cap; black blouse and tunic; girdle; navy blue scarf; white breeches; cobbât.

87 *ALGERIA: c. 1850*
JUIF MARCHAND DE LIVRES. *Coloured engraving*
Rubens (ii) 1721
Brown caftan; *striped tunic, coloured turban and mules without heels* (paboudj).

85

86

87

88

and down the front, by means of small metal buttons or wire hooks. Loose drawers reaching to the knees and black leather slippers complete the dress; but when the weather is cold, they throw over all the burnoose or cloak, made of black wool. In winter they sometimes wear stockings but generally the legs are naked. Their girdle, like the rest of their dress, must be black, red is strictly forbidden.

'The dress of the Jewish women consists of a fine linen chemise with long loose sleeves, over this a large robe, covering the body, but leaving the neck and breasts bare: it is made of cloth or velvet, according to the circumstances of the wearer, and is embroidered round the edges; their petticoat is commonly dark green superfine cloth, embroidered with gold, and reaching no farther than the knee; the legs are bare, and the feet thrust into little slippers, so small that they just cover the toes, and can scarcely be kept on in walking. Round the waist they wear a sash of silk and gold, the ends of which, adorned with little metallic plates, are suffered to hang loosely behind, so that when they move these make a tinkling noise. The unmarried women wear the hair plaited in different folds and flowing down the back; they have a very graceful method of twining a wreath of wrought silk round the head and weaving it behind into a bow. The married women cover their heads with a flowing silk handkerchief, and occasionally use the sarmah or tiara, made of gold or silver, and set with precious stones, over which they throw a veil on going out, so managed as to draw across the back of the head, shoulders, and lower part of the face, leaving uncovered their eyes, of which they make excellent use. They have an extravagant

88 *ALGERIA: c. 1850*
JUIVE D'ALGER. FEMME MARIÉE. *Coloured engraving*
Rubens (ii) 1717
On her head is a çârma covered by a white veil the ends of which are draped round the front of her body. She wears a ghlîla the short sleeves of which pass through the openings in the black djubba which descends to the ground.

89 *MOROCCO: 1781*
Engraving. From Höst
FIG. 1. MOROCCAN JEW
All Jews wore black caps, burnous and slippers but the caftan could be of other colours. The Jews had to drape the burnous over the shoulder as shown.
FIG. 2. RABBI
He has no special costume but wears larger and wider sleeves, a red sign on the black burnous and usually a blue handkerchief around the cap.
FIGS. 3 AND 4. JEWESS
She wears a wrap-over skirt of red or green material, the outer pointed end of which is decorated with gold or silk embroidery; belt; corselet; plastron with long sleeves joined together on the back and red or embroidered shoes with heels. This is an early and everyday version of the keswa el kbira.

Fig: 1

Fig: 2

89

Fig: 3

Fig: 4

90

passion for ornaments; and every Jew who can afford it, tricks out his wife and daughters in the greatest profusion of earrings, bracelets, anklets, rings, chains and other trinkets. On Sabbaths and feast days, they appear in all their finery, the men putting on their best clothes, which, however, cannot vary in form and colour from the appointed standard, while the women, who are less restricted, set no bounds to the splendour of their attire. . . .

'Their robes are generally of blue wool or silk, embroidered with gold; over this they place a spencer without sleeves, also ornamented with gold, and closed by golden buttons. The sarmah is festooned with a silk shawl enriched with pearls, and supplied with a long golden streamer, which, attached like a tail to its inferior parts, hangs as low as the ground. The slippers are velvet or Morocco leather, embroidered with gold wreaths, but the legs are always naked. Bracelets of gold or silver adorn their arms; finally necklaces of pearl, or coral, or golden chains, set off the snowy whiteness of the neck, which they take particular pains to expose as much as possible. The Jewish women do not paint figures on their faces and limbs, as the Moorish women do, but they stain with henna the nails, the palms of the hands and soles of the feet, and renew this once a week; they, some of them, blacken their eyebrows, and all use depilatories, which are applied in the form of a paste at the bath, and come off bringing with them superfluous hairs.

'Bathing is a frequent practice; a Jewess, even in moderate circumstances, will go to the bath at least twice a month. The Jewish children are clothed in the same manner as their parents, but

90 *ALGERIA: c. 1850*
ENFANS JUIFS. *Coloured engraving*
Rubens (ii) 1716
The boy has on his head a chéchia *slightly pointed with a pompon on top as worn by Moslem children. His outer garment is a* ghlîla *which is worn over a* bed'iya. *He has shoes without heels* (cobbât). *The girl wears a* ghlîla *the short sleeves of which pass through the* djubba, *the long outer dress.*

91 *MOROCCO: c. 1830*
[CIRCUMCISION] *Engraving*
Jewish Theological Seminary
The men bearded in black caps, belted tunics, burnous *and breeches; the women with false hair, the long tails of which hang down their backs.*

92 *MOROCCO: 1836*
REV. DR M. EDREHI. A NATIVE OF MOROCCO. *Engraving*
Rubens (ii) 88
The rabbi, who settled in London, wears a turban and Eastern costume. A seal is suspended from his neck.

93 *MOROCCO: Tetuan c. 1880*
[JEWESS FROM TETUAN] *Photograph*
From Lenz
Her dress is a particularly fine example of the keswa el kbira, *showing the ornate gold embroidery work for which the Jewish women of Tetuan were renowned.*

91

92

93

the girls are not allowed the sarmah and the golden tails until they are marriageable, that is when they have attained their ninth year. The boys wear their hair long up to the same period, and have it almost dyed red with henna. The children of the rich are dressed sufficiently well, and both sexes wear caps of blue velvet, adorned with a number of gold coins, proportionate to the wealth of the family. As many as a hundred gold sequins may be at times seen thus disposed.'

Finally he gives this description of a Jewish bride:

'In the afternoon her female friends congregate to pay their compliments to the bride, and dress her out in the finest clothes which she possesses. The inside of her hands, and the soles of her feet are stained red; red figures are traced on her forehead, on each cheek a triangle of the same colour with a gold leaf in the centre. Her eyebrows and the edges of the lids are blackened, her hands, from the bend of the wrist to the tips of the fingers, covered with black lines drawn zig zag; her head-dress is tricked out with jewels and lace, finally they throw over her shoulder a kind of scarlet silk mantle, embroidered with gold.'[25]

By the middle of the nineteenth century most of the restrictions on Jewish dress had disappeared. In some cases if a turban was worn it had a tassel attached to it as a distinction and old men still wore the traditional costume.[26]

AUTHORITIES: D. de Haedo; *Jewish Encyc.*   P. B. Lord; G. Marçais; A. Salamé.   *(See Bibliography)*

Morocco

As in most parts of North Africa where Jews are found, the Moroccan community is of ancient origin and dates back well before the Arab conquest. Its costume, which is particularly interesting, has been carefully studied and few travellers have failed to comment on the beauty of the Jewish women and the richness of their dress.

An early reference to the black clothing common to all Jews in North Africa is contained in a twelfth-century edict of the Sultan Moulay Ismaël from which it appears that all his subjects had hitherto worn black slippers; thenceforth they were to be worn only by Jews.

According to Leo Africanus (*c.* 1526) the Jews of Fez wore black turbans or a cap with a piece of red material attached and were not allowed shoes.

Lancelot Addison, who was chaplain at Tangier from 1662 until 1670 when it belonged to Charles II, has left the best account of the Moroccan Jews of that time. They wore, he said

'little black brimless caps, as the Moors red which they seldom move in greeting one another. They likewise, as the Moors, go slipshod (i.e. in slippers)

[25] Lord, 98 ff. 127–8
[26] The Victoria & Albert Museum possesses a *çârma* and other examples of Jewish North African dress.

and wear linnen drawers and vest over which they put a loose garment called a *ganephe* which differs only in colour from the *mandilion* or *albornoz* which the Moors bestow upon the Christians when they are redeemed from slavery. This *ganephe* is a black square piece of coarse hair-stuff closed at the cross corners and all round it is a large Thrum which at first sight looks like their Religious Fringes whereof we shall have occasion in due time and place to discourse. The Jews in this Continent much resemble the Spaniard and Portuguez in their stature and complexion . . .'[27]

In a description of a wedding Addison mentions that it was a custom for the bridegroom to send the bride a girdle with a silver buckle and for him to send her one with a gold buckle. The wearing of a silk sash or girdle was a Moorish custom.

Another writer gives a very similar account of the men's dress at this period:

'The Jews wear a shirt, drawers, a black close-coat or Caffetan and over it a black or dark coloured kind of cloak which they call Albernous made with a cowl like a Fryers Frock but there hangs down strings at the end of the cowl and at the bottom. They have a black cap, black pumps and slippers.'[28]

Höst supplies information about Jewish costume at the end of the eighteenth century [Plate 89]. All the men wore black caps, *burnous* and slippers. Only the *caftan* could be of a different colour. The rabbis had no special dress but wore, as a distinction, larger

and wider sleeves, a red mark on their black *burnous* (as mentioned by Leo Africanus) and usually a navy handkerchief round the cap.

The women, who according to Höst were usually good-looking, did not differ much in their dress from the Moorish women. They wore an open skirt of red or green material, the outer pointed end of which was embroidered in gold or silk; the skirt was held together by a belt above the waist. The sleeves of the jacket were usually knotted behind the back. The slippers were red or embroidered and had heels. In the streets half the face was exposed to distinguish them from the Moorish women.

In 1789 William Lempriere, an army physician attached to the garrison at Gibraltar, travelled through Morocco, where he had been invited in order to attend the Emperor's son. In the towns he usually stayed at a Jewish house in the Mellah (the only part of the town where a Christian was safe) and as he was held almost as a prisoner long after he wished to leave he had plenty of opportunity of studying the Jews. He was shocked at the way the Moors treated them, particularly as they were the only mechanics

[27] Addison, 10–11 [28] *A Letter concerning the . . . countries of Muley Arxid*, 1671. Quoted by Mendelssohn

G

94

and were responsible for the whole of the commerce of the country including the Treasury and Mint.

The men shaved their heads close and wore their beards long. They were dressed in a black cap, black slippers and instead of the Moorish *haick* an *alberoce (burnous)*, a cloak made of black wool. They were not allowed to carry a sword or ride a horse.

Lempriere writes at length about the Jewish women.

'The dress of the Jewish women consists of a fine linen shirt, with large and loose sleeves, which hang almost to the ground; over the shirt is worn a *caftan*, a loose dress made of woollen cloth, or velvet, of any colour, reaching as low as the hips, and covering the whole of the body, except the neck and breast, which are left open, the edges of the caftan being embroidered with gold. In addition to these is the *geraldito*, or petticoats, made of fine green woollen cloth, the edges and corners of which have sometimes a gold ornament; this part of the dress is fastened by a broad sash of silk and gold, which surrounds the waist, and the ends of it are suffered to hang down behind, in an easy manner; when they go abroad, they cover the whole with the *haick*, the same as used by the Moorish women. The unmarried Jewesses wear their hair plaited in different folds, and hanging down behind; and to this they have a very graceful and becoming method of putting a wreath of wrought silk round the head, and tying it behind in a bow. This dress sets off their features to great advantage, and distinguishes

94 *MOROCCO : Tangier 1828*
A JEWISH WEDDING AND A DANCE. *Engraving*
From Beauclerk
The bride on a dais at the back; the other women in ceremonial dresses with the typical sleeves tied at the back.

95 *MOROCCO : c. 1830*
COSTUME OF THE BARBARY JEW HAWKER IN GIBRALTAR. *Drawing*
Beard; black cap; navy blue burnous; *striped silk girdle; white shirt with long sleeves; white trousers; mules.*

96 *MOROCCO : Fez c. 1940*
MARRIED JEWESS OF FEZ. *Drawing*
Besancenet Plate 52
Another example of the ceremonial costume, keswa el kbira. It differs slightly in cut from the Rabat model, and the muslin sleeves, which are much shorter, are turned back below the elbow and pinned to the inside of the short sleeves of the corselet. The decoration, which is much simpler, includes the stylized hmames *designed to ward off the evil eye. The coiffure is also simpler than that at Rabat. It comprises a frame,* sfifa, *to which are attached long strands of black silk imitating hair separated into two long bands falling behind on to the shoulders. Her chin and cheeks are painted with little white and red dots following an ancient Arab custom. This costume which was painted from authentic documents is now extremely rare as most of the examples were destroyed when the Mellah was sacked in the 1912 riots.*

97 *MOROCCO : c. 1900*
[BERBER JEWS FROM THE ATLAS MOUNTAINS] *Photograph*
From Jewish Encyclopædia *ix : 23*
In native costume with girdles
All are bearded

95

96

97

98

them from the married women, who cover their heads with a red silk handkerchief, which they tie behind, and over it place a silk sash, leaving the ends to hang loose on their backs. None of the Jewish women have stockings, but use red slippers, curiously embroidered with gold. They wear very large gold ear-rings at the lower part of the ears, and at the upper, three small ones set with pearls or precious stones; their necks are loaded with beads, and their fingers with small gold or silver rings; round each wrist and ancle are fixed large and solid silver bracelets; and the rich have gold and silver chains suspended from the sash behind.

'Their marriages are celebrated with much festivity for some time previous to the ceremony, and the intended bride, with all her female relations, go through the form of having their faces painted red and white, and their hands and feet stained yellow, with an herb named *henna*. A variety of figures are marked out with a needle, and this herb, which is powdered and mixed with water into a paste, is worked in, and these marks continue on the hands and feet for a long time.

'The Jewesses of this empire in general are remarkably fair and beautiful. They marry very young, and when married, though they are not obliged to hide their faces in the street, yet at home they are frequently treated with the same severity as the Moorish women. Like the Moors, the Jewish men and women at Morocco eat separate; and the unmarried women are not permitted to go out, except on particular occasions.'[29]

An English officer, Capt. G. Beauclerk, in an account of his travels through Morocco in 1826–7 has much to say about the Jews.

98 *MOROCCO: Rabat c. 1940*
MARRIED JEWESS OF RABAT. *Drawing*
Besancenet Plate 51
She wears the ceremonial dress, keswa el kbira, *reserved for weddings and special occasions. It is made entirely of velvet usually of green or blue for towns in the interior and claret for the coasts and south. The open skirt,* jelteta, *which is wound from left to right is heavily decorated with gold braid. A corselet, deeply scooped out, with short sleeves,* gonbaiz, *also loaded with gold braid has attached to it by silver filigree buttons the* plastron *(front) made of the same velvet and covered with gold embroidery. Long wide sleeves,* kmam tsmira, *are attached to the short sleeves of the* plastron *and the ends are pinned on the back. Her coiffure, the* sualef, *consists of two fringes of imitation hair made of black silk thread with two plaits,* dlalat, *which hang down in front. It is held in place by means of a tiara set with pearls and precious stones and has a silk scarf,* festul, *attached to it which hangs down behind as far as her heels. Her eyes are blacked with* khol *and she is heavily made up.*

99 *MOROCCO: Goulmima c. 1940*
JEWESS OF GOULMIMA. *Drawing*
Besancenet Plate 57
This woman from the Mellah of Goulmima close to Tafilelt wears a red dress. From the immense coiffure two corkscrews of wool can be seen hanging from the wig on to the shoulders.

[29] Lempriere; 185–6

99

100

100 *MOROCCO: Tiznit c. 1940*
JEWESS OF TIZNIT. *Drawing*
Besancenet Plate 53
This ceremonial dress is a compromise between that of the towns and the Anti-Atlas. It is also of velvet, red or green, but the flounced skirt, jelteta, retains the style of the saya. The corselet is called qaftan. The coiffure, tijajin d-mahduh, is particularly remarkable. It is like a coif made of silver thread with five grooves decorated with cloisonné enamel. The hair made from black cows' tails falls in two bands across the forehead. Attached to the hair is the festul, *a red scarf with gold brocade.*

101 *MOROCCO: Tafilelt c. 1940*
JEWESS OF TAFILELT. *Drawing*
Besancenet Plate 55
The Jewish women in the Mellahs of the Atlas Mountains and the oases of the south dress like their neighbours and this dress is similar to that worn by Berber women. Is is only the coiffure which shows Jewish influence. It is called grun *(horns) from its unusual shape and is made of two skeins of thick wool tightly bound with little plaits to form a horn on each side of the face. These are firmly held by bands of material and a bonnet. This woman is in her outdoor dress and her coiffure is covered with a large veil of white muslin decorated with little flowers.*

101

102

About their houses in Tangier he writes:

'The interior of them is kept particularly clean by means of continual whitewashing ... the floors are often paved with small coloured tiles ... and the houses generally consist of four rooms one storey high only built long and narrow and so arranged as to enclose a small square yard ... At the ends of the rooms are ranged the beds on a raised wooden platform and in the centre of the floor are mats made of coloured rushes whereon sit with their legs tucked up, the inmates of the house.'

The Jewish women, he says:

'are kept under no restraint and are exceedingly courteous to strangers. They have generally bad figures but pretty faces; indeed many of them are very beautiful. Their complexion is high coloured but their skin very fair.'

He visited a Jewish house where they were celebrating the last day of the nuptials of one of the daughters of the house:

'... we found the bride, a very handsome young woman with a pair of coal-black eyes, seated on the nuptial bed ... It is impossible to conceive anything more splendid than her dress. Her head was encircled with a very wide flat turban of white muslin and gold, the body of her gown, her jelick, and her slippers of red Morocco leather, were all most tastefully embroidered with gold, and a thin transparent veil of flowered muslin hung negligently about her person.' [Plate 94.]

'At Mogadore many of the richer Jews wore round hats and some indeed frock coats, an affectation borrowed from the Europeans. The Sultan charged a substantial fee if anyone required

102 *MOROCCO: Todrha c. 1940*
JEWESS OF TODRHA. *Drawing*
Besancenet Plate 58
Her wig, sualef, *probably the most curious in Morocco contains 30 to 40 cows' tails made into two enormous headbands weighing nearly a kilo. Down the centre is a string of small silver ornaments and coloured stones crowned by a band of silver coins and a silk handkerchief. From the wig hang two long thick skeins of heavy wool on to the shoulders.*

103 *INDIA: c. 1830*
JEW. *Drawing*
Man and woman of the Bnei-Israel
Rubens (ii) 1639
The man is clean shaven but has side locks and a black skull cap. He wears a brown waistcoat with long sleeves, violet jacket with short sleeves, Muslim-style white cotton trousers and Indian-type wooden shoes. The woman wears a white scarf over her hair, the front part of which is exposed. Her white upper garment is Western in style. Her red skirt is in the sarong style of Malaya and Indonesia which is only occasionally seen in India where it is known as mekhala.

104 *MOROCCO: 1936*
[MOROCCAN JEWISH COIFFURES]
From Jouin

1 *Fez Meknes Séfrou*	6 *Ouarzazat*
2 *Taroudant*	7 *Dades Todra*
3 *Tiznit Talaint*	8 *Figuig*
4 *Rabat Tetuan*	9 *Todra*
5 *Midelt*	10 *Tafilalet*

103

104

1   2   3   4

5   6   7   8

9   10

105

exemption from wearing the black skull cap.'[30]

In November 1846 Alexandre Dumas was asked by the Ministre de L'Instruction Publique to visit North Africa and the account of his travels which he subsequently published contains much about the Jews. It includes an entertaining description of a Jewish wedding at Tangier. The following are extracts:

'We went through into a square courtyard surrounded by houses, each with its own balcony or roof garden overlooking the court. In the centre grew an enormous fig-tree, every branch densely packed at the moment with Moorish and Jewish children. On two sides of the courtyard were benches for spectators, and here we were offered seats. A third side, giving on to the street, was occupied by three musicians, one playing a violin which he held before him like a 'cello, and two others beating basque drums. The fourth side, the façade of the bride's home, was thronged by a dozen Jewish matrons arrayed in their richest robes, while through the doorway we glimpsed fifteen or twenty other women guests.

'At six we made our way back to the bride's home, but found the nearby streets now so crowded by curious sightseers that without David's help I doubt whether we should have been able to pass. Scarcely had we seated ourselves at one end of the room, which was about twenty feet long and not more than eight feet wide, when red damask curtains at the far end were drawn back to reveal the bride surrounded by her maids. She was brought to the middle of the assembly and perched upon a raised chair, where the

105 *MOROCCO : Beni-Sbih c. 1940*
JEWESS OF BENI-SBIH. *Drawing*
Besancenet Plate 60
She is dressed like the Berber women. The Jewish women of the valley of the Dra do not wear wigs but have little curls of ostrich feathers on their temples.

106 *INDIA : Bombay 1842*
BNEI-ISRAEL OF BOMBAY. *Engraving*
From Wilson
The author gives this description of the Bnei-Israel : 'The Bnei-Israel in their physiognomy resemble the Arabian Jews, thought they view the name Yehud, *when applied to them, as one of reproach. They are fairer that the other natives of India of the same rank of life with themselves ; but they are not much to be distinguished from them with regard to dress. They have no* shendi, *like the Hindus, on the crown of their heads ; but they preserve a tuft of hair above each of their ears. Their turbans,* angrakhâs, *and shoes are like those of the Hindus ; and their trousers like those of the Musalmans. Their ornaments are the same as those worn by the middle class of natives in the Maratha country. Their houses do not differ from those of other natives of the same rank'.*

107 *INDIA : Cochin 1860*
WHITE JEW. *Wood engraving*
From Lawson

108 *MOROCCO : Tililt c. 1940*
JEWESS OF TILILT. *Drawing*
Besancenet Plate 59
Her wig is covered by a diadem made of small silver plaques. The black and red designs on her face are similar to those of the Berber women.

[30] Beauclerk, 14, 21, 231

106

107

108

109

matrons surrounded her, removed her red veil
and began to dress her hair. When that was
arranged to their liking, they piled upon it three
separate head-dresses, one above the other; then
a sash twisted round like a stove-pipe on which
they finally placed a coronet of red velvet shaped
into points like the crown of the Frankish kings.
'Then a woman with a fine brush began to
paint her eyelids and eyebrows with kohl, while
another came up to her with two pieces of gilded
paper prepared with cochineal. In turn the
attendant licked each of these, placed it, all damp,
upon the bride's cheek, gave a few rubs which
could certainly have been lighter and gentler,
and by this simple process created a vivid car-
mine blush, while the poor victim never opened
her eyes or made the slightest movement. Now
she was led from her chair to a kind of throne
placed upon a table, and there she sat, still as a
Japanese statue, while her brother, candle in
hand, displayed her to all the world, and the
women of the family fanned her with their handkerchiefs. For half an hour we all waited in
silence, hearing nothing except the raucous
laughter of Moorish women every ten minutes or
so, and an undulating thread of sound from the
musicians in the courtyard.'[31]

The traditional costume of the Jewish
women of Morocco, now rare, is still seen
today at weddings and ceremonial occasions.
Fortunately about 30 years ago when it
was not so scarce it received the most careful
study at the hands of Mlle. Jouin and M.
Besancenet and even then the costume was so

109 *INDIA: c. 1864*
DAVID SASSOON. *Engraving*
Rubens (i) 344
*David Sassoon (1792–1864) the founder of David Sassoon &
Co., the Bombay banking house, was a native of Baghdad and
wears the traditional Baghdadi costume.*

110, 111, 112 *INDIA: Cochin c. 1880*
[WHITE JEWS OF COCHIN] *Photographs*
From Racinet
*The man is bearded and dressed in Indian Islamic style but the
material which is silk would not be worn by Muslims. The
women's dress is Spanish in style and has affinities with the
ceremonial dress of the Jewish women of Morocco. The
costume on the left is particularly fine being made entirely of
gold brocade with lace sleeves. Both women wear a Tahli gold
chain. Their hair is only partly covered.*

[31] Dumas, 49–52

110

111

112

expensive that most brides had to borrow it from a relative. It bears no resemblance to other Moroccan costume and is different to the ceremonial Jewish costume of Algeria and Tunis, which is derived from Moslem dress. It is in fact Spanish costume and there can be little doubt that it was brought to Morocco when the Jews were expelled from Spain in 1492. It has changed very little since the time when it was first described by Höst.

Even more interesting than the costumes are the coiffures; for the Jewish women, like those of Eastern Europe, observed the practice of cutting their hair on marriage and replacing it with a wig. But Morocco produced a variety of regional styles of remarkable originality which cannot be paralleled elsewhere [see Plate 104].

The basic ingredients of the Jewish ceremonial dress, the *keswa el kbira*, are:

1. The *gonbaiz* (*qasot* at Tetuan), a corselet with short sleeves deeply scooped out at the bosom and held below the breasts by means of silver filigree buttons and button holes of gold braid. This is the garment Lempriere calls a *qaftan*.

2. A *plastron* (front) designed to cover the opening in the corselet. It is separate and is tied by laces at the back. It is called *punta* at Tetuan, *peto* at Tangier, *ktef* at Rabat, Salé and Mogador; *ujha* at Fez, Meknès and Sefrou.

3. *Kmam*, wide muslin sleeves called *mangos* at Tetuan. In the coastal towns they are made up of six or eight bell-shaped panels joined by gold braid. They are voluminous, quite separate and are turned back and fastened with pins on the back. In the towns of the interior, they are straight or pointed and are partly fastened to a calico blouse.

4. The *jelteta (geraldeta)*, a wide wraparound skirt entirely open in front. It measures more than 3 metres at the bottom and is secured at three points, one on each side and one behind and by slanting seams at the hips. It is not gathered like the *saya*, a skirt which took its place during the present century.

5. A sash belt of silk and gold brocade called *hezam* in the coastal towns and *kusaka* at Fez, Meknès and Sefrou. It is folded three times breadth-wise and wound twice round the body.

The jacket, the skirt and the *plastron* are made of velvet. In the interior of the country they were usually green, but on the coast and at Marrakech they were red. The lavish decoration in lace and gold embroidery which follows traditional design incorporates

113

stylized stars to ward off the evil eye, and doves as emblems of good luck.

This ceremonial costume was given to a Jewish bride by her father as part of her dowry. She wore it first for her wedding and kept it the rest of her life for great occasions like weddings and circumcisions. For less important occasions she had a dress of the same style but in dark colours and decorated with *appliqués* of red silk.

The costume shown by Lenz [Plate 93] is believed to be from Tetuan, which had the reputation for producing the finest embroidery made by Jewish needlewomen.

A very comprehensive collection of Moroccan Jewish costume is to be found in the Bezalel Museum, Jerusalem.

India

The Jews of India are divided into four main groups: the Bnei Israel, who are coloured, the White Jews originating from Baghdad, the Black Jews of Cochin and the White Jews of Cochin. The last of the Cochin Jews emigrated to Israel in 1961.

The earliest known drawing of a man and woman of the Bnei Israel [Plate 103] dates from about 1830. The man is clean shaven but has side locks *(peoth)* and wears a black

AUTHORITIES: L. Addison; G. Beauclerk; J. Besancenet; A. Dumas; P. Ewald; J. Goulven; G. Höst; *Jewish Encyc.*; J. Jouin; W. Lempriere; S. Mendelssohn; S. Purchas. *(See Bibliography)*

skull cap and Moslem-style white cotton trousers. The woman's upper garment is Western in style and she has a rather unusual sarong type of skirt. Her hair is not completely covered and the married women were apparently allowed to show their hair. Later in the nineteenth century it seems that the men wore turbans. Elderly men wore beards; young men, side locks [see Plate 106]. At the beginning of the present century the men had abandoned turbans and were wearing a round embroidered cap [Plate 113].

The Baghdadi Jews, some of whom came from other parts of the Levant besides Baghdad, wore the Turkish *djubba* and *entari* with a turban. They all had long rounded beards [Plate 109].

The following description of the White Jews of Cochin was written in 1860:

'their features are fine if not (especially with the elders) noble; broad and high forehead, roman nose, thick lips, generally however concealed by a most luxuriant, jet-black, curly beard'. For synagogue they wore fine clothing: 'robes of silk, velvet or satin of a scarlet, blue, green or amber tint with costly shawls wrapped around the head and waist and a lavish display of gold chains and buttons made of English Sovereigns . . . their costume does not at all resemble that of the natives of India.' On ordinary occasions they wore a white cotton skull cap, jacket, waistcoat and trousers. The jacket had full sleeves, breast pockets and twelve silver buttons fastened by a fine silver chain attached to the topmost hole. The writer observes that the Jewish women had recently adopted gowns of silk, linen or chintz but that formerly their costume was very different and far more pleasing. [32]

This description is accompanied by an illustration of a White Jew [Plate 107].

The women's ceremonial dresses, which are made of silk and gold brocade are Western in cut, and have a strong affinity with the Spanish costumes of the Jewish women of Morocco [Plates 110–112].

According to the *Jewish Encyclopædia*, the weekday dress of the White Jews at the beginning of the present century was the same as that worn by the natives, but the Black Jews were covered only from the waist down, wore a red handkerchief on their heads, and had side locks *(peoth)*. In the synagogue the White Jews wore a turban, a shirt, a jacket with twelve buttons (as described by Lawson) and over this a *djubba*, and trousers. All married women wore a gold chain with a peculiar coin in the middle called *tahli*.

[32] Lawson, 120

AUTHORITIES: *Jewish Encyc.*; C. A. Lawson; J. Wilson. *(See Bibliography)*

The Western World

Mediaeval period

Nothing is known about Jewish costume in Europe during Carolingian times and the earliest reference to Jewish dress is a complaint by Archbishop Agobar of Lyon in 826 about the lavishness of the clothing given to Jewish women by princesses and the wives of courtiers. In 839, Deacon Bodo, a German, became a convert to Judaism and to mark the occasion adopted the name of Eleazar, allowed his hair and beard to grow and put on a military belt. Whether the last item had any significance is not known but a belt or girdle later became a Jewish characteristic in certain countries, notably in Poland.

Fur-trimmed garments were a feature of Jewish dress, according to a ninth-century writer who reported that 'Pope Nicholas was so strongly opposed to Arsenius, Bishop of Orta, because of his effort to introduce Jewish furred garments *(judaicae peluciae)* that the Pope threatened to exclude him from the Palatine procession unless he vowed to discard the clothes of the superstitious race and agreed to walk in the procession wearing the priestly fillet'.[1]

The tradition for a distinctive form of dress based ultimately on *Leviticus* xviii: 3 is stated specifically in the *Shulchan Aruch*:

'We should not follow the ways of idolaters; nor wear a garment which is characteristic of them; nor grow locks of hair as they do; nor shave at the sides and leave hair in the middle; nor shave the hair in front of the head from ear to ear and leave a pigtail . . . Anyone close to royalty who must wear their clothes and be like them may do so.'[2]

The gloss on this states that any fashion which serves a useful purpose such as the distinctive dress of physicians or anything worn out of respect is permitted.

There are frequent reminders of this Jewish attitude towards dress in the regulations and Sumptuary Laws issued by various communities.[3] The *Takanot* (laws) of the communities of Speyer, Worms and Mayence in Germany passed at Rabbinical Synods held during the thirteenth century contained the following provisions:

'No one shall cut his hair in non-Jewish fashion or shave his beard either with a razor or such a manner as approximates the effect of a razor nor shall one wear long hair.

[1] Straus, 61
[2] *Shulchan Aruch: Yoreh Deah.* 178 paras. 1 and 2. The *Shulchan Aruch*, the most important code of rabbinic Judaism, was written in the sixteenth century. The reference to idolaters (literally: 'worshippers of the stars') rather than Gentiles is significant.
[3] The Sumptuary Laws are dealt with below.

115

114

114 *ENGLAND: 1275*
[ENGLISH JEW]
Drawing
British Museum. Cottonian Ms. Nero D2
He wears a gardecorps *with Jewish Badge and hood.*

115 *FRANCE: Thirteenth century*
[JESUS AND THE THREE PHARISEES]
Miniature. Ms. Francais 403
Bibliothèque Nationale
The leading Pharisee wears a curious version of the Jewish hat resembling a helmet (cf. Pl. 117). Full length tunics with hoods; cloaks fastened on shoulder.

116 *N. FRANCE: Eleventh century*
[JOEL]
Miniature. From the Stavordale Bible *British Museum Add. Ms. 28106–7.*
The earliest illustration of the Jewish hat. Mediaeval tunic with cloak fastened over shoulder.

116

117

117 *ENGLAND: 1233*
[CARICATURE OF ENGLISH JEWS]
Drawing
Public Record Office. Ms. dated 1233
In mediaeval times under the Angevin Kings the Jews and all their possessions belonged to the King who made himself responsible for their protection, and the chief Jewish centres had royal castles where they could seek shelter in times of danger. One of these centres was Norwich and the caricature shows various Jews on the ramparts of the castle there. Isaac of Norwich, the wealthiest Jew of his day, who is bearded, wears the royal crown of Henry III, possibly in order to indicate that he is the King's property. It has three fleurs-de-lys on it like the crown on the first Great Seal of Henry III. The figure on the left, clean-shaven and holding a pair of scales, wears a pointed hood. Mosse-Mokke, also clean-shaven, wears a spiked hat shaped like a helmet, which is possibly the Norman-French version of the Jewish hat [cf. Plate 115]. Abigail wears a barbette and fillet, the contemporary head-dress. Her hair, in a long plait, hangs down her back.

118 *N. ITALY: Verona twelfth century*
[MOSES WITH THE TABLETS OF THE LAW]
Panel from bronze doors of San Zeno illustrating two different types of Jewish hat.

118

H

119

'No child of the Covenant shall dress after the manner of Gentiles nor wear sleeves.

'No one shall go to the synagogue otherwise than with a cloak or topcoat but one should not wear a *suckenis*'[4] *(sargenes)*.

These communal directives were reinforced by numerous Dress Regulations issued by the Church or by the civil authorities the earliest of which, made at Perpignan in 1295, required Jews to wear a cape. From the same place in 1396 Juan I of Aragon ordered the Jews of Murviedro to wear a *gramalla* (long outer gown) or other garment covering the toes in addition to a yellow badge on the breast. In Majorca the Jews were required to wear attached to their hood a cowl the length of a palm shaped like a funnel and sewn up to form a point [perhaps as shown in Plate 124]. In addition they had to wear a *gramalla*. At Valladolid in 1412 the laws were given more precisely:

'All Jews and Moors are to wear long robes over their clothes as low as their feet, and are not to wear cloaks; and in all cities, towns and places, they are to wear their distinctive red badge. But it is my pleasure, that, to avoid the dangers they might otherwise incur in travelling, they may wear the clothes they now have, as well as in the places they may go to.

'That all Jewesses and Moriscas of our kingdoms and dominions, shall, within ten days from

119 *FRANCE: Fourteenth century*
[THE JEWISH BADGE]
Miniature. Ms. Francais 820 f 192
Bibliothèque Nationale
The bearded figure on the right is a Jew and wears a red and white badge, blue hood, pink cloak and green inner tunic.

120 *ENGLAND: Thirteenth century*
[A PROPHET]
Fresco
From a drawing in the Victoria and Albert Museum
Tristram Pl. 40(d)
Prophet with Jewish hat coloured green. From the soffit of the arch in the North wall, Holy Sepulchre Chapel, Winchester Cathedral.

121 *SPAIN: Fourteenth century*
[DESCENT FROM THE CROSS. *Detail*]
Fresco. Chapel of Santa Lucia, Tarragona, Spain.
Jewess in the dress prescribed by law and wearing the Jewish Badge.

122 *SWEDEN: c. 1210*
[WORSHIP OF THE GOLDEN CALF]
Fresco
Bjaresjo Church, Skane, Sweden
Examples of the Jewish hat in Sweden. The men are bearded and wear mediaeval tunics with cloaks fastened over one shoulder. One is bareheaded.

[4] Finkelstein 233 ff.

120

121

122

124

123

125

123 *ENGLAND: Fourteenth century*
[ZACHARIAH AND HIS WIFE]
Drawing
British Museum
From the Holkham Bible Picture Book; *facsimile ed.*
1954 folio 18
Detail from the Birth of John the Baptist. Zachariah wears an unusual collar not found on any other costume in this series and perhaps denoting a priest. His wife wears a cloak over a surcoat. Her head-dress is the contemporary fillet *and* barbette *and her hair is padded and netted. The drawing is probably based on an earlier model made prior to the expulsion of the Jews from England in 1290.*

124 *SPAIN: Fourteenth century*
[JACOB'S BODY CARRIED TO CANAAN]
Miniature. From the Sarajevo Hagadah;
The monastic type of dress prescribed for Spanish Jews. Full length gowns with capes. The hoods are pointed. Labels, characteristic of academical dress and consisting of two tongues of white fur or silk, appear to be part of the hood. They are not the same as bands which developed from the seventeenth century falling collar.

125 *SPAIN: Castile thirteenth century*
[JEWS OF CASTILE]
Miniature. From Las Cantigas *No. 25 f. 38*
El Escorial, Madrid
Composed for Alfonso X of Castile (1252–84), the Cantigas, of which there are 194, describe the miracles performed by pictures or images of the Madonna. Most of them are illustrated by miniatures, many of which show attempts by Jews to desecrate a picture or image as the result of which they are drowned, burned or converted.
The Jews wear a curious form of the Jewish hat with three-quarter length tunics and cloaks.

126

126 *GERMANY: c. 1375*
[THE JEWISH HAT]
Miniature
Dresdener Sachsenspiegel
From Amira
*Jew and priest, the latter being identified by his tonsure. The
Jew is bearded, wears a pointed hat and carries a sword.*

127 *GERMANY: Thirteenth century*
SÜSSKIND DER JUDE VON TRIMBERG
Miniature
University Library, Heidelberg
*Süsskind of Trimberg, a Jewish troubador, stands before the
bishop wearing a Jewish hat, beard and long hair.*

127

128

this date, wear long mantles, reaching to their feet, and cover their heads with the same. Those who act contrary, for so doing, are to forfeit all the clothes they may have on to their under garment.

'That no Jew or Moor, ten days after this date, shall wear cloth of which the entire suit costs upwards of thirty maravedis; those who act contrary shall, for the first offence, forfeit the apparel they have on to the shirt; for the second, lose all their clothes and receive a hundred lashes; and for the third, all their property shall be confiscated to my treasury. But it is my pleasure that, if they choose, they may make coats and cloaks of the clothes they now possess.

'Henceforward Jews and Moors are not to shave their beards, or have them shaved with razors or scissors; nor trim nor cut the hairs, but are to wear them long as they grow naturally, as they were formerly accustomed. Any person who acts contrary hereto, shall receive a hundred lashes, besides paying a fine of a hundred maravedis for each time he transgresses.'[5]

A regulation of the City of Cologne dated 8 July 1404 required Jews and Jewesses of all ages to wear distinctive dress and in particular laid down the following rules:

'Sleeves on coats and jackets may not exceed half an *elle* in width.

'Collars on jackets and cloaks may not exceed one finger in width.

'No fur may be shown at top or bottom of clothing.

'Lace is permitted on sleeves only.

'Cuffs on sleeves may not exceed the length of

128 *GERMANY: 1329*
[SEAL OF S. MOSES]
From Revue des Études Juives *IV. 279*
The Jewish hat was frequently used as the design on Jewish seals in mediaeval times. See Monumenta Judaica *B. 160.*

129 *GERMANY: Rhineland end of fourteenth century*
[THE EMPEROR, HENRY VIII, GRANTING PRIVILEGES TO THE JEWS OF ROME]
Miniature
Staatsarchiv, Coblenz
Only the leader of the Jewish delegation (the rabbi?) is bearded. All wear full length tunics under long gowns and a late form of the Jewish hat.

130 *GERMANY: Fifteenth to sixteenth centuries*
[THE JEWISH HAT IN GERMAN HERALDRY]
Coat of arms of the German family of Jude
An example of 'canting' arms. Names like this probably originated as nicknames and are not necessarily evidence of Jewish ancestry.
From Sibmacher

131 *GERMANY: Fourteenth century*
[THE JEWISH HAT]
Miniatures
From the Leipzig Machsor
In the upper miniature the crowned female figure appears to be wearing the Jewish Badge—a unique example of it being shown on a Jewish Ms.
In the lower drawing the reader wears full length tunic, hood and tallith with pendulous tsitsith. The others have Jewish hats with full length tunics and cloaks.

[5] Lindo 199 ff.

129

JUDE.

130

131

Franckfurter Juden Stättigkeit.
Form der Hüth.

127

132

133

134

132 *BELGIUM: 1528*
[A JEWISH ASTRONOMER]
Woodcut. From Tabule Perpetue . . . *Louvain 1528*
*Among a group of astronomers the Jew is recognisable by his
beard and frilled collar. Jewish astronomers were prominent in
mediaeval times and the celebrated Alfonsine Tables prepared
by two Jews of Toledo were still being consulted by Galileo in
the seventeenth century.*

133 *GERMANY: Fifteenth century*
[JEWISH HAT]
Engraving
From Schudt
Form of hat prescribed by the laws of Frankfurt a/m.

134 *GERMANY: Fifteenth century*
[THE SEDER]
Drawing
Hebrew Ms. Hagadah
Hebrew Union College, Cincinnati
*The husband is bearded and wears the Jewish hat prescribed
by the laws of Frankfurt a/m [see Plate 133]. The wife wears
a contemporary bonnet called* gebende.

135 *GERMANY: 1509*
[JEWISH OATH]
Woodcut
Rubens (ii) 1596
The Jews wear full length gowns and chaperons *with the
Jewish Badge on left arm or shoulder.*

136-7 *GERMANY: Worms sixteenth century*
TRACHT DER JUDEN ZU WORMS
Drawings
Stadtarchiv, Worms
Monumenta Judaica B.139
The man in a cloak and chaperon, *the woman in a cloak and
veil. Both wear the Jewish Badge.*

138

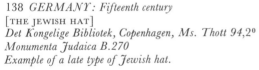

138 *GERMANY: Fifteenth century*
[THE JEWISH HAT]
Det Kongelige Bibliotek, Copenhagen, Ms. Thott 94,2°
Monumenta Judaica B.270
Example of a late type of Jewish hat.

137

139

the hand.

'Coats must be fringed and must reach the calves.

'Cloaks may not be open on both sides and must reach to within a hand's width of the ground.

'Hoods of males over the age of 13 must be one *elle* in length, the shoulder collar one and a half *elles* but not wider than one-eighth.

'Silk shoes are forbidden both indoors and outdoors.

'Unless close-cropped, the hair above the lobe of the ear may not be cut.

'No child over the age of three may wear open clothing.

'A girl may not wear a hair ribbon worth more than 6 gulden or wider than two fingers.

'On ordinary days women may not wear more than one ring on each hand nor one worth more than 3 gulden.

'On ordinary days they may not wear gold belts nor a belt wider than two fingers.

'On festivals they may wear belts up to 2 silver marks in value and two rings up to 6 gulden in value.'[6]

One result of the various Dress Regulations was that the Jews with their hoods and long cloaks were frequently mistaken for monks and to prevent this the Council of Albi in 1254 issued the following decree:

'And since by reason of the round capes which Jews generally wear the respect due to the clergy is seriously impaired for they (the clergy) use round capes habitually we decree with the approbation of this Council that in the future Jews shall

139 *GERMANY: 1530*
[GROUP OF JEWS]
Woodcut
Rubens (ii) 1044
They wear cloaks open at sides, Jewish Badge and chaperon with liripipe.

140 *GERMANY: 1588*
JEW OF THE PALATINATE
JEW OF FRANKFURT A/M
UNMARRIED JEWESS
JEWESS DRESSED FOR SYNAGOGUE
Engravings
From C. Rutz, Sacri Romani Imperii Ornatus, *1588*
The Jew of the Palatinate wears a cloak with chaperon and liripipe. The Jew of Frankfurt has a Jewish Badge on his cloak and wears a hat. Both women wear the orales, the Jewish veil, which had two blue stripes, and the married woman has the regulation topcoat for synagogue. She also wears the Badge.

141 *GERMANY: 1530*
[CEREMONY OF TASHLIK]
Woodcut
Rubens (ii) 1046
Men wearing chaperons with liripipes; the women wearing chaperons except for one whose head-dress is a gebende.

142 *ITALY: 1556*
[GRACIA NASI AGED 18]
Bronze Medal
By Giovanni Paolo Poggini of Ferrara
From a reproduction

[6] *Monumenta Judaica* B.313

Iudæi vestitus in Palatinatu commorantis. Iudæi vestitus Francsurti ad Mœnum habitantis.

Virgo Iudæa inquilina Germaniæ superioris. Iudæa in Synagogam abiens religionis ergo.

41

40

141

142

143

144

143 *ITALY: Mantua early fifteenth century*
[DANIEL NORSA AND HIS FAMILY]
Painting
Church of Sant' Andrea, Mantua
Both men are bearded and wear the Jewish Badge. For an explanation of the painting see C. Roth, History of the Jews in Italy, *Philadelphia, 1946, 174.*

144 *PORTUGAL: c. 1465-7*
[DETAIL FROM THE VENERATION OF ST VINCENT]
Tempera and oil on oak by Nuno Goncalves
Museu Nacional de Arte Antiga, Lisbon
The picture, which is a polyptych, shows members of the Court and Portuguese society praying before St Vincent, the patron saint of Portugal. The rabbi, holding a Hebrew book, wears a cylindrical black hat and gown. On his breast is the Jewish badge, a six-pointed star in red.

145 *AUSTRIA: Vienna 1551*
[DECREE OF EMPEROR FERDINAND I]
Friedburg Stadtarchiv XIIᶜ
Monumenta Judaica B.359
All Jews are required to wear a yellow ring (as shown) on the left side of the chest or dress within one month of coming to reside in any town.

146 *AUSTRIA: Prague 1514*
[KIDDUSH]
Woodcut
From Seder Zemirot Ubirchat Hamazon Prague 1514
Statni Zidovske Museum, Prague
The woman's coiffure is the gebende *which covers the chin and holds the head-covering in place. The men on each side of her wear a* barrette *and a coat with a deep collar called* schaube. *All are in contemporary costume.*

Wir Ferdinand von Gottes genaden Römischer / zů Hungern vnd Behaim ꝛc. Künig / Infant in Hispanien / Ertzhertzog zů Osterreych / Hertzog zů Burgundi / Steyr / Kärndten / Crain / vnnd Wirtemberg ꝛc. Graue zů Tyrol ꝛc. Embieten N. allen vnd yeden Prelaten / Grauen / Freyen / Herrn / Rittern / Knechten / Landßhaubtleüten / Haubtleüten / Vitzthumben / Vögten / Pflegern / Verwesern / Ambtleüten / Burgermaistern / Richtern / Räthen / Burgern / Gemainden / vnnd sonst allen andern vnsern Vnderthanen vnd getrewen / Geystlichen vnd Weltlichen / in was Wirden / Stand / oder Wesen die allenthalben in vnsern Landern / Obern / vnnd Vordern Osterreichischen Fürstenthumben vnd Landen / Obrigkeiten vnd gebieten gesessen sein / denen diser Vnser offner Brief fürkhumbt / den sehen / lesen hören / oder des sonst in ernnerung kommen / Vnser Gnad vnd alles gůts.

145

146

not dare to wear round capes. They may how-ever wear capes with long sleeves the sleeves being as long as the capes but in these sleeves there must be no folds or creases.'

The outstanding characteristic of Jewish costume in mediaeval times was the pointed Jewish hat or *Judenhut*. In its simplest form it was a plain cone similar to the Persian *kalansuwa* worn by non-Believers in Moslem countries from which presumably it originated and it could have been introduced to Europe either through Spain or Byzantium. It was probably accompanied by another Persian garment, the *caftan*, which with its girdle also became a feature of Jewish dress.

The first illustrations of the Jewish hat are found on miniatures in the Stavordale Bible which are not later than 1097 [Plate 116], but the more characteristic form is found on the bronze doors of San Zeno at Verona in Northern Italy which are twelfth century or possibly earlier. Two different styles are seen on the same panel [Plate 118], which makes dating difficult, but the hat must have been a distinctive Jewish feature well before the twelfth century by which period it had become established as a universal symbol of Jewry equivalent to the *Magen David* of modern times. It was proudly displayed on

Hebrew manuscripts, unlike the Jewish Badge which was a mark of degradation and was always bitterly resented. It was commonly used as a design for a Jewish seal, as seen on the thirteenth-century seal of the Augsburg Jewish community[7] and the fourteenth-century seal used by Swiss Jews. The Badge, better known as a mark of distinction than the Jewish hat because it survived much longer, must have been inspired by its much earlier Moslem counterpart but is not known in Europe prior to the thirteenth century.

The Fourth General Council of the Lateran, which ruled that Jews should in future be distinguished by their clothing, was more important than any of the Church Councils which preceded it and remained for generations the authority on all disputed points of canon law. It was summoned by Innocent III, the Pope who supported King John of England against the Barons over Magna Carta.

The Council opened on 1 November 1215 and the Pope announced that the two chief tasks before him were the recovery of the Holy Land and the reform of Catholic life.

[7] This is in the later form shown on Pl. 138. See R. Grunfeld, *Ein Gang Durch Die Geschicte Der Juden in Augsburg*, Augsburg, 1917.

Of the seventy canons, No. 68 requires Jews to wear a distinctive dress:

'In some Church provinces a difference in dress distinguishes the Jews and Saracens from the Christians, but in certain others there is great confusion and they cannot be distinguished. Thus it happens at times that through error Christians have relations with Jewish and Saracen women and Jews or Saracens with Christian women. Therefore, that they may not, under such pretext resort to excusing themselves in the future for the excesses of such accursed intercourse, we decree that such (Jews and Saracens) of both sexes in every Christian province and at all times shall be distinguished in the eyes of the public from other peoples by the character of their dress. Particularly, since it may be read (in *Numbers* xv: 37–41) that this very law has been enjoined upon them by Moses.'[8]

The sixth canon ordered the bishops for each ecclesiastical province to meet annually in order to secure observance of the laws and to remedy abuses. These provincial councils thenceforth became the chief legislative bodies with regard to Jewish dress, the popes themselves for the next two centuries being more occupied in fighting for their very existence with various Catholic princes.

The Council did not specify what distinctions were required nor did it indicate where action had to be taken but presumably England, France and Spain were the chief countries it had in mind. Drawings of the thirteenth century from these countries showing groups of Jews, with the Jewish hat being worn only in isolated cases, indicate that the hat was falling into disuse and this must be the reason why the Badge was enforced in those countries first. In Germany on the other hand, either because the *Judenhut* remained in use or because of the various Dress Regulations already mentioned, the Badge was not enforced until much later except at Mainz and Erfurth. At Gnesen in the Kingdom of Poland, at Breslau, at Strasbourg and in Austria in 1267, the Jews were ordered to retain the pointed hat *(pileus cornutus)*.

The Jewish hat was accompanied by a beard and usually a long coat. When Süsskind Von Trimberg, a troubador, became a Jew, he announced that he intended to grow a beard and wear a Jewish hat and a long coat. He is thus portrayed in a miniature from the thirteenth-century *Manesse Codex* at Heidelberg, except that his cloak with its ermine collar is similar to that worn by the seated bishop [Plate 127].

In Germany, particularly, the *Judenhut* was part of the Jew's regulation costume.

[8] Grayzel, 335

147

148

147 *ITALY: Padua 1594*
JUDAEUS MERCATOR PATAVINUS
Engraving
Rubens (ii) 1728
Although described as a Paduan, he speaks Yiddish. He wears the Jewish barrette.

148 *POLAND: Fourteenth century*
[FLIGHT TO EGYPT]
Painting on glass
Wolowslaw Cathedral
From Schipper
Joseph wears the pointed Jewish hat.

149 *ITALY & GERMANY: Seventeenth century*
[JEWISH MARRIAGE RINGS]
A *Gold filigree with blue and white enamel. Italian early seventeenth century.*
B *Gold. South German late seventeenth century.*
C *Gold. Italian early seventeenth century.*
D *Gold. Italian early seventeenth century.*
Jewish Museum, London.

149

150

151

150 *POLAND: Twelfth–thirteenth century*
[POLISH JEWS]
Miniature from a Ms. in a Church at Krushvitz
From Schipper
One in knee length, remainder in full length tunics and mantles.
One bareheaded, remainder in round caps; all bearded.

151 *POLAND: Fifteenth century*
[JEWISH PROSECUTOR]
Painting
St Catherine's Church, Cracow
From Schipper
He wears the pointed Jewish hat.

I

152

The Schwabenspiegel, a code of law compiled about 1275, states specifically that Jews must wear one and the miniatures in the Sachsenspiegel dating from about 1375 show that it still remained their recognised headdress [Plate 126].

The colour of the hat was usually yellow, like its counterpart in Moslem countries, but on manuscripts a variety of colours is found including red and white.

For heraldic purposes the Jewish hat was employed for 'canting' arms, i.e. coats of arms in which the armorial bearings contain an allusion to the name of the family. Thus the arms for *Jüdden, Juden* or *Judei* of Westphalia are given as 'De gules à trois chapeaux d'argent' and those of *Judels* of Holland as 'D'argent à trois chapeaux de juif de gules les cordons de sinople' while the crest was 'Un chapeaux de l'écu sans cordon' [Plate 130]. The arms for *Joeden* include a figure wearing the Jewish ruff.[9]

As stated above the Badge was first introduced into those regions where the Jews were not readily recognisable by their dress: England in 1218, Castile in 1219, Provence in 1234, the Papal States in 1257. By the fifteenth century it was an accepted

152 *POLAND: Lithuania 1815*
LITHUANIAN JEWESS
Engraving
From R. *Johnson,* Travels through Part of the Russian Empire, 1815
Rubens (ii) 1651
The feature of the dress is the head scarf terminating in three tails [see p. 136].

153 *POLAND: 1703*
EIN POLNISCHER JUD
Engraving
Rubens (ii) 1732
Large round hat; robe buttoned to neck with frilled collar and girdle; caftan and mules.

154 *POLAND: 1765*
JUIF POLONOIS
Etching
Rubens (ii) 1733
Fur hat, long robe with girdle and cloak. Perhaps the dress for Sabbath.

155 *POLAND: 1765*
FEMME JUIVE POLONOISE
Etching
Long dress and coat. Her head is covered with a scarf tied at the side.

[9] Sibmacher. Cf. the arms of the English family of *Jew*: 'Argent a chevron between 3 Jews' heads couped at the shoulder proper' (B. Burke, *The General Armory,* London 1878). A coat of arms made up of 3 Jews' hats white on an azure ground appears in a German fourteenth-century *Machsor* in the Ambrosian Library, Milan.

153

154

155

156

157

156 *POLAND: 1817*

ENFANS JUIFS
From Norblin
Rubens (ii) 1740
The girl has her hair uncovered. Both boys wear caftans with girdles and both have their heads covered, the one on the left with a yarmulka, the other with a streimel.

157 *POLAND: 1817*

FEMME JUIVE
Engraving
From Norblin
She wears a scarf over a head-covering trimmed with lace, the typically Jewish plastron, the brüsttüch, and somewhat elegant shoes.

158

159

158-59 *POLAND: 1817*
POLISH JEW IN HIS SUMMER DRESS
A POLISH JEWESS
Drawings
Victoria & Albert Museum
Identical drawings made in 1817 by Sir Robert Ker-Porter
are to be found in the British Museum (Add. Ms. 14758(2))
and there are copies in the author's collection. Sets of drawings
like these, showing national costume, were produced for tourists
in countries which lacked facilities for engraving.
The man wears a yellow yarmulka *with red embroidery,*
white tunic with girdle, blue breeches, yellow stockings and
mules. The woman, whom Ker-Porter calls 'a dark beauty',
has two items of dress which distinguished the Jewish women
of Poland: the forehead band (stirnbindel) *and the plastron*
(brüsttüch). *The former is described as being made of velvet*
and gold bound with a border of pearls.

160

requirement all over Europe but enforcement was lax partly because many rulers were prepared to grant exemption for a money consideration—a constant source of complaint by the Church Councils which continued to re-issue the regulations with monotonous frequency.

The Badge was usually in the shape of a ring hence the name, *rouelle* (wheel), and the regulation colour was yellow, although other colours existed and in parts of France the Badge was a circular piece of cloth parti-coloured red and white [Plate 119]. In some places it took the form of a patch of yellow or red cloth. At Schaffhausen in 1435 it was the shape of a Jew's hat.

The usual position was the breast but sometimes it had to be worn on the shoulders, the back or the hat or in two positions.

In Portugal, in 1289, the Jews were required to wear a yellow hat or hood which was replaced in 1391 by a red star [see Plate 144]. A similar badge was imposed on the Jews of Verona in 1480.

In England the Badge consisted of a piece of white material shaped to represent the Tablets of the Law—hence the name, *tabula* [Plate 114]. This shape is found nowhere

160 *POLAND: 1817*
JUIF REVENANT DE LA SYNAGOGUE
Engraving
From Norblin
Rubens (ii) 1739
He wears a fur trimmed hat (spodic), *coat with girdle, Sabbath cloak without sleeves, white stockings and buckled shoes.*

161 *POLAND: Nineteenth century*
[COSTUME OF POLISH JEWESSES]
Brüsttücher (Plastrons)
Bezalel Jewish National Museum, Jerusalem.

162 *RUSSIA: 1843*
FAMILLE JUIVE DANS SON INTERIEUR
Lithograph
From Scènes Populaires Russes *1843-4*
The women wear a tall bonnet tied with a scarf which seems to have been a feature of Jewish women's dress at this period. The boy on the right has long peoth *and wears an* arba kanphoth.

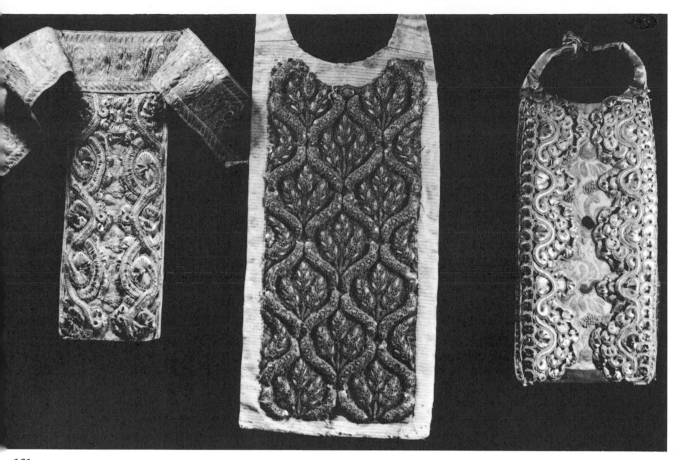

161

162

163

164

163 *RUSSIA: Crimea. Karaites 1840*
KARAIMES
Lithograph
From Demidov
The author makes this comment:
'The Karaimis, wedded to commerce like their brethen everywhere, are of sedentary habits with gentle and friendly manners
and their attention to their clothes and homes are characteristic
of their sect. One learns that their reliability and honesty in
business have won them great esteem. It is a really distinguished
race and their nobility is stamped on their faces. The young men
seen in the picture gather together every evening to chat and
gossip.'

164 *RUSSIA: Crimea. Karaites 1840*
JEUNE FEMME KARAIME
Lithograph
From Demidov
*Demidov was invited by the Karaite Chief Rabbi to his home
where he was shown the women's apartments and he gives this
description of their dress:*
'The costume of the young woman has an elegant air. A dress
of striped silk clinging closely to her figure has not been spoiled
by any foreign influence. A wide belt resting on the hips is
joined in front by a rich clasp made of two silver plaques finely
worked. A scarf forming a turban adorns the beautiful hair
hanging in tresses. Around her neck is a gold collar and a thin
silk cravate and she wears a yellow satin jacket with black
embroidery. Her shoes are the ungainly slippers of the country.
This sweet figure gently stooping through maidenly shyness and
supported by two children made a delightful picture.

165

165 *RUSSIA: Odessa 1837*
NEGOCIANTS ET MARCHANDS ISRAELITES, ODESSA 7 AOUT
1837
Lithograph
From Demidov
According to the author the principal merchants foregathered
every evening at the Richelieu Café where most of the business
was conducted. All wear caftans *with girdles and tall felt*
hats with wide brims or fur-trimmed hats but in either case a
yarmulka *is worn beneath.*

166 *RUSSIA: c. 1845*
ENFANS JUIFS
Lithograph
From Costumes de la Petite Russie
The boy has peoth *and wears a black* caftan *and a fur-*
trimmed hat.

166

167

else. Used at first as a means of extracting money the wearing of the Badge was more strictly applied after 1253 when Henry III issued a fresh series of Statutes based on ecclesiastical canons, thus falling into line with the decrees of Innocent III. By the *Statutum De Judeismo* of 1275 the nature of the Badge was more clearly defined and its colour changed to yellow.[10]

Usually the Badge applied to men, women and children but a special distinction for women was a veil with two blue stripes. This requirement is found in a Papal Bull of 1257 which remained in force at Avignon until the fifteenth century, was repeated by the Council of Ravenna, 1311, and by the Council of Cologne, 1442, by which time it applied all over Germany. The veil, known at first by its simple mediaeval Latin name, *oralia* or *orales*, had by 1326 become a pointed veil called *cornalia* or *cornu*, which is presumably the same pointed veil as the Jewish women of Augsburg were ordered to wear in 1434. In Germany, where it was called *flieder*, *sendelbinde* or *riese*, it remained the typical head-dress for Jewish matrons until the seventeenth century or perhaps later.[11] In 1360 all Jews of Rome save physicians

167 *POLAND: 1846*
LE CHASSIDE ET SA FEMME
Engraving. Rubens (ii) 1754
He wears a tall fur hat, white smock with tsitsith *on its corners, girdle, white stockings, black caftan. His wife wears the typical Jewish plastron, the* brüsttüch, *and an unusual head-dress.*

168 *POLAND: Lithuania 1846*
LE JUIF LITHUANIEN AVEC SA FEMME ET SA FILLE
Engraving. Rubens (ii) 1753
He wears a fur-trimmed hat (spodic), *a black caftan with girdle, white stockings and slippers. The daughter is allowed to show her hair but the wife's head is completely covered.*

169 *POLAND: Warsaw 1846*
LE JUIF DE VARSOVIE ET SA FEMME
Engraving. Rubens (ii) 1751
He wears a tall fur-trimmed hat, black caftan with girdle, white stockings and shoes. His wife has a crown of pearls.

170 *POLAND: Lithuania 1846*
LA BOURSE LITHUANIENNE
Engraving. Rubens (ii) 1752
All the Jews wear black caftans with girdles. Two types of hat are shown and one example of the yarmulka *worn under the hat.*

[10] 'And every one of them that is past seven years of age shall wear a Badge in form of two Tablets of yellow Taffety six fingers long and three fingers broad upon his upper garment.' D'B. Tovey, *Anglia Judaica*, 1738, 202.
[11] Probably the same as the *Viereckiger Schleier* mentioned below. At Speyer and Frankfurt a/m in the fifteenth century the regulations required Jewish women to wear two blue stripes on their clothing as at Rome and veils were not mentioned (see *Monumenta Judaica*, B. 315, 319).

168

169

170

171

were required to wear a red *tabard* and the women a red petticoat. By a Papal decree of 1555 Jewish women were ordered to wear a head-dress made of yellow cloth. Numerous other variations existed.

Although the pointed Jewish hat went out of use in Europe during the Middle Ages, a hat of a specified colour remained a Jewish mark of distinction in the Papal States until the French Revolution. Clement VII on 13 June 1525 substituted a yellow hat for the Badge and, although withdrawn after protests from the Jews, it was reintroduced later by Paul IV, in 1555. He ordered the Jews of the Papal States to wear a green *barrette* but allowed them to wear a black hat in towns and villages where they were accustomed to trade.[12]

In Venice also a yellow hat was obligatory and it is recorded that in 1528 the Council of Ten granted permission to Jacob Mantino, the physician, to wear the *barrette noire*, only after the French and English ambassadors, the papal legate and other patients had pleaded for him.[13]

In Austria an order issued in 1551 by the Emperor Ferdinand I referred to the fact that the Jews of his empire had abandoned their distinctive costume and required them

171 *POLAND: Cracow c. 1850*
JUDENWEIB AUS DEM KRAKAUER-KREISE GALIZIEN
Lithograph
Jewish Theological Seminary
She wears the Jewish brüsttüch *and an unusual head-dress.*

172 *RUSSIA: Odessa 1856*
THE JEWS' WALK AT ODESSA
Engraving
Illustrated London News, *1856*
Men and women in traditional dress.

173 *POLAND: Brody 1891*
[GALICIAN JEW]
Drawing by J. Pennell
Illustrated London News *12 December 1891*
Galician Jew with long beard and peoth *wearing* streimel *and* caftan.

174 *GERMANY: Worms seventeenth century*
[MICHAEL GERNSHEIM]
Drawing
Jewish Encyc. *XII. 563*
The Judenbischof *(official head of the Jewish community) at Worms is bearded and wears a round cap with turned-up brim and clerical bands.*

[12] *Revue Des Etudes Juives* xxxvi, 53 ff.
[13] *R.E.J.* xxxvii, 30 ff. *Jewish Encyc.*

172

173

174

175

176

Neüe Schwarm geister=Brüt.

178

175 *GERMANY: Frankfurt a/m 1614*
[PLUNDER OF THE GHETTO]
Engraving
Rubens (ii) 1581
The Jews wear the Jewish barrette, *the Jewish ruff and the*
Badge. Their women wear the ruff, the Badge and bonnets
with ears.

176 *GERMANY: c. 1650*
NEUE SCHWARM GEISTER-BRUT
Engraving
A satire attacking Quakers and other sects. The Jew (No. 4)
is identified by his ruff.

177 *GERMANY: 1692*
[PREACHING IN SYNAGOGUE]
Woodcut
From Minhagim, Dyhernfurth, 1692
The men in berets (barrettes), ruffs and sleeveless gowns
(sarbals) all of which were characteristically Jewish. The
rabbi's gown has deep sleeves.

178 *GERMANY: 1694*
[TALLITH, TEPHILLIN AND ARBA KANPHOTH]
Drawing
From Encycl. Judaica X
The man wears tallith *and* tephillin; *the boy has the flat*
round Jewish hat (barrette) *and* arba kanphoth. *Both*
wear the Jewish ruff.

to wear a yellow badge [see Plate 145].

The Jewish hat was not the only article of clothing which entered into Jewish tradition. The *sargenes* or *kittel*[14] which dates from Talmudic times is a shroud consisting of a white linen over-garment reaching the feet with voluminous sleeves, a collar laced in front, a girdle of the same material and a cap to match. It was worn on New Year and the Day of Atonement, for weddings and by the head of the house for the Seder meal during the feast of Passover. Passover was originally a New Year festival and the wearing of a special costume for New Year was a common practice in ancient times. At the Greek spring festival of Anthesteria shrouds were worn in order to disguise the individual and feign death while the divine powers were fixing his fate during the coming year.[15]

Gifts between bride and bridegroom known as *sablonoth (sivlonoth)* go back to Talmudic times. An account of a fifteenth-century wedding in the Rhineland describes how on the eve of the wedding the bride and bridegroom exchanged gifts through the rabbi. The bride received a gold-studded belt, a veil, a *kurse*[16] and a garland: the bridegroom, a sash, a ring and a pair of shoes. The bride's mother gave her a silver belt.

On the wedding day the bridegroom appeared in his Sabbath clothes but he also wore the German *gugel* or *kappe (chaperon)* and ashes on his head in mourning for Zion while the bride was enveloped in a *sargenes*. She also wore the *kurse* given to her by the bridegroom and a *turmkrone* (tower crown) consisting of a golden headband set with little towers. During the ceremony the bridegroom wore a *tallith* which the rabbi also wrapped round the bride.

The *sivlonoth* marriage belts, which remained a feature of Jewish women's dress until modern times [see Plate 203], were a survival from the mediaeval marriage belts originally worn in many parts of Europe.

AUTHORITIES: I. Abrahams; J. Aronius; K. von Amira; J. Bauer; A. Berliner; A. Boeckler; J. Charles-Roux; C. W. & P. C. Cunnington; M. Davenport; *Encyc. Judaica*; J. Evans; L. Finkelstein; A. C. Fox-Davies; H. Gold; H. Graetz; S. Grayzel; M. Grunwald; D. de Haedo; J. N. Hahn; W. N. Hargreaves-Mawdsley; P. Hughes; *Jewish Encycl*; *Jüdisches Lexikon*; B. Kisch; G. Kisch; S. Krauss; M. Letts; E. H. Lindo; J. G. Lovillo; J. R. Marcus; *Monumenta Judaica*; Müller & Schlosser; H. Norris; H. G. Richardson; U. Robert; E. v. Rünsberg; J. Sibmacher; R. Straus; E. W. Tristam; *Universal Jewish Encycl*. See *Bibliography*.

[14] In German, *sarge* = coffin; *kittel* = smock or blouse
[15] Segal, 146-7
[16] A kind of blouse with fur hem and long sleeves which were turned back to show the silk lining.

Russia and Poland

An ecumenical council held at Breslau in 1266 decreed that the Jews living in the bishopric of Gnesen in Poland should wear a special hat, and the Council of Ofen in 1279 required the Jews to wear a red badge. The Jewish hat appears on two mediaeval paintings from Poland [Plates 148–51]. A different costume is seen on a miniature of the twelfth or thirteenth century [Plate 150] showing a group of bearded Jews in the tunics and cloaks characteristic of Western Europe, but probably unfamiliar in Poland where native mediaeval dress consisted of a *caftan* and a fur hat. It was this native costume which the Jews subsequently adopted and it was probably to restrain a movement in this direction that the Piotrkov Diet of 1538 passed the following decree:

'Whereas the Jews disregarding the ancient regulations have thrown off the marks by which they were distinguishable from the Christians and have arrogated to themselves a form of dress which closely resembles that of the Christians, so that it is impossible to recognise them, be it resolved for permanent observation that the Jews of our realm, all and sundry, in whatever place they happen to be found, shall wear special marks, to wit, a *barrette* or hat or some other headgear of yellow cloth. Exception is to be made in favour of travellers, who, while on the road,

shall be permitted to discard or conceal marks of this kind.'[17]

By paragraph 12 of the Lithuanian Statute of 1566 it was provided that 'the Jews shall not wear costly clothes nor gold chains nor shall their wives wear gold or silver ornaments. The Jews shall not have silver mountings on their sabres or daggers. They shall be distinguished by characteristic clothes; they shall wear yellow hats and their wives kerchiefs of yellow linen in order that all may distinguish Jews from Christians'.[18]

Thus it seems that the wearing of swords by Jews was accepted. The requirement that they should dress differently was reinforced by a rabbinical edict issued in 1607 prohibiting the adoption of Christian dress, and the Lithuanian Jewish Council between 1623 and 1762 also issued various sumptuary laws affecting dress.

Caftans with fur-trimmed hats were the basic features of Polish and Russian national dress in mediaeval times and were still being worn in 1576.[19] As the trend towards

[17] Dubnow 1, 77–8   [18] *Jewish Encyc*. viii, 126
[19] As seen on an engraving of the Russian ambassadors and their staff at the Regensburg Congress of 1576. There is a framed copy in the London Library. Illustrations of mediaeval Polish costume are given in Eljasz.

K

179

180

179 *GERMANY: Hamburg 1690*
[KETUBAH]
Drawing
In possession of Mrs Gomperts Teixeira de Mattos
Wedding of Samuel, son of Isaac Senior Teixeira, and
Rachel, daughter of Abraham Senior de Mattos, on 17 June
1690. The Sephardim of Hamburg, like those of Amsterdam
and London, wore contemporary dress; the men have full-
bottomed wigs and the women wear fontanges.

180 *GERMANY: c. 1700*
EIN JUD DER NACH DER SYNAGOG GEHET
Engraving
Rubens (ii) 1598
Dressed for synagogue in a sleeveless cloak (sarbal) *on which*
is fixed the Jewish Badge in the shape of a heart. He has the
round black hat (barrette) *and pleated ruff typical of German*
Jewish costume.

181

Western dress developed among the Polish upper classes, their original dress was gradually taken over by the Jews, and by the eighteenth century it had become their characteristic costume.

The features of this dress varied in different parts of Poland and included a skull-cap *(yarmulka, keppelche* or *kappel)*; a cap with ear flaps *(lappenmütze* or *klapove hitl)*; a high fur hat trimmed with plush called *spodic* (Polish =saucer) or one made of sable *(kolpak)*. The *mosalka* was a silk skull cap worn especially by Hasidim and a fur cap called *duchowny* was reserved for scholars. In Galicia the characteristic hat for the Sabbath was the *streimel* (Polish *stroj* = costume), a saucer shaped hat with a flat fur brim which in the case of rabbis was made from 13 sables' tails. Gaily decorated *yarmulkas* were worn in the synagogue.[20]

After the French occupation of Poland in 1812 some Jews adopted Western dress, but the majority had become fanatically attached to their Polish costume and a Russian Council of State in 1840 found that the special dress worn by Jews helped to keep them apart. This resulted in an imperial *ukase* issued 1 May 1850 prohibiting *peoth* (side locks) and the wearing of a distinctive Jewish

181 *GERMANY: c. 1700*
DIE JÜDIN NACH DER SYNAGOG GEHEND
Engraving
Rubens (ii) 1599
She is very simply dressed. The feature of her costume is the large ruff, while the cloak was obligatory for synagogue wear. Her bonnet completely covers her hair indicating that she is married.

182 *GERMANY: Frankfurt a/m 1703*
FRANCKFURTHER JUD UND JÜDIN
Engraving
Rubens (ii) 1584
For everyday wear the man wears a broad-brimmed hat, knee-length coat and gown. His lace collar has become typically Jewish as has the woman's ruff and her bonnet with its curious ears.

[20] For illustrations see Goldstein & Dresdner.

Abbildung der Jüden und ihrer Weiber Trachten. in Fürdt. 1706.

183

184

183 *GERMANY: Fürth 1705*
[COSTUME OF JEWS AND THEIR WIVES]
Engraving
From Boener
The women in their distinctive Jewish ruffs with sleeves to match and cloaks. They seem to be wearing frets as head-dress. The man in the centre wears a ruff but the one on the right (the rabbi?) is in a plain collar, a Jewish barrette, a tunic buttoned down the front and a sleeveless cloak.

184 *GERMANY: Nuremberg 1731*
[WEDDING]
Engraving
From J. J. Beck
The mothers of the bride and bridegroom in frets. Men and women wear the Jewish ruff.

185 *GERMANY: 1716–17*
[THE SEDER]
Drawing
From an Hagadah dated 1716–17
Hebrew Union College
The master of the house wears the prescribed dress for this occasion, the sargenes. The other men have contemporary three-cornered hats and white bands. The wife is elegantly dressed.

Die Jüden=Ordnung wird gemacht.

186

form of dress in any part of the empire, although aged Jews could wear out their old garments on payment of a tax.[21]

In April 1851 a further order was made forbidding Jewish women to shave their heads on marriage. When Alexander II visited Poland in 1870 and saw Hasidic Jews still wearing *peoth* he gave instructions that the law should be rigorously enforced.

The following description of the dress of Polish Jews is given by Hollaenderski (1846):

'a long coat or frock coat in black cloth edged in front with velvet and fastened from the neck to the waist; a wide belt, socks, shoes or slippers; a skull cap; a hat with a wide brim most of which is shaped like a sugar loaf or cut-off cone with a deep edge of sable or other fur. Finally a greatcoat as long as the under-coat. All this normally in black and in light material like silk. Rarely does a Jew, even if rich, possess more than two outfits, one for working day the other for Sabbath so that the colour gradually becomes unrecognisable and the whole costume gradually turns to rags. Eventually it is patched in many colours. The hair is normally shaved and hidden under the skull cap but there is a long side curl on each side; the beard is unkempt and reaches to the chest. The women dress like the Polish women. Their head is shaved and covered with a kerchief knotted in various ways. The rich ones wear little crowns decorated with pearls and diamonds and long earrings.'[22]

186-7 *GERMANY: Frankfurt a/m 1714-8*
[JEWISH COUNCIL ISSUING DRESS REGULATIONS: A WEDDING]
Engravings
From Schudt
The men in the usual barrettes *and ruffs; the women wear the* viereckiger schleier *(square veil) which had become a distinctive feature of their dress and they are in their synagogue capes and ruffs.*

188 *GERMANY: Fürth 1705*
[JEWISH BRIDE]
Engraving
From Boener
The bride wears a short jacket (probably the kürse *presented by the bridegroom) and a marriage belt. The other women are in their synagogue cloaks and have enormous Jewish ruffs.*

[21] Similar attempts to compel Jews to adopt Western dress were made in Austrian Poland. Item 1216 in Catalogue 67 (1964) of A. Rosenthal Ltd., of Oxford was a Permission from the Austrian police at Lemberg dated 8th July 1840 for a Jewish oculist to live outside the ghetto provided he did not wear Jewish dress.
[22] Hollaenderski, 224-5

132

Die Braut geht hier mit großem Pracht.

187

188

189

190

191

189 *GERMANY: 1734*
[Jew dressed for prayers]
Engraving
Rubens (ii) 1150
He wears tallith, arba kanphoth *and* tephillin.

190 *GERMANY: 1733*
[wedding]
Woodcut
From Minhagim, *Frankfurt a/m 1733*
The women wear the viereckiger schleier *(square veil) and
ruffs, both typical features of Jewish dress. The men are in*
barrettes *and ruffs.*

191 *GERMANY: Nuremberg 1731*
[a business transaction]
Engraving
From J. J. Beck
*The Jews are bearded and wear deep pleated collars, cloaks
and unusual* barrettes *with ribbed frames.*

192 *GERMANY: Fürth 1734*
[wedding procession]
Engraving
Rubens (ii) 1170
*The mothers of the bride and bridegroom wear their marriage
belts and each is in a* fret *head-dress made of silver and gold
trellis work. The other women are in horned head-dresses,
ruffs and synagogue cloaks. The men wear the typical Jewish
dress of the period.*

193 *GERMANY: Nuremberg 1731*
[prayers for new moon]
Engraving
The barrettes, *cloaks and ruffs are similar to those worn by
Jews in other parts of Germany.*

A

B

192

NÜRNBERG

193

194

grofser Herren Gunst misbraucht mit bösen
Wen Geitz und Ubermuth auch Wollust anspornt

Although the Jewish women dressed like the Polish women their wardrobe included certain distinctive types of head-dress: a crown of diamonds and pearls [see Plate 169] or a lace cap adorned with flowers and birds (*kupkeh* or *binde*): and there were various types of forehead-band (*stirnbindel* or *stern-stichl*) some like diadems of pearls, others made of bands of satin, silk or velvet with tinsel or pearl embroidery and fastened by two ribbons. Another distinctly Jewish item of dress was the *brüsttüch* or plastron which also lent itself to elaborate and expensive decoration.[23] [See Plate 161.] A favourite pose for Jewish women was with one or both hands concealed by the *brüsttüch* [Plate 157].

The picture of Lithuanian Jewesses [Plate 152] is accompanied by the following un-flattering description of the Jewish women of Orcha, a town on the west bank of the river Dnieper:

'(they) are clad in a most ridiculous and gaudy dress of silken rags; on their head is a large white napkin rolled round with 3 tails hanging over their shoulder; and under this head dress a kind of flapping cover of pearls with dangling steel ornaments hangs over the ear and forehead. The body is covered with a loose silk vest and a large petticoat of the same; the arms are hid in long loose shirt-sleeves terminated with a deep worked

194 *GERMANY: 1738*
[JOSEPH SÜSS OPPENHEIMER]
Mezzotint
Rubens (ii) 2166
The costume of a Court Jew. He is fashionably dressed with a wig and is clean-shaven.

195 *GERMANY: 1738*
[JEWISH OATH]
Etching
From Buxtorf, Synagoga Judaica, Frankfurt a/m 1738
The oath, more judaico, by German law had to be taken bare-headed standing on a sow's hide. The Jewish ruff is the only typical feature of the dress.

196 *GERMANY: Frankfurt a/m 1774*
BEER DANN, SCHUTZ-JUDE
Etching
Rubens (ii) 2044
The dress of a protected Jew.

197 *GERMANY: 1785*
BLUMCHEN FRIEDLANDER
Engraving
Rubens (ii) 2063
Although married she wears her hair uncovered as a sign of emancipation.

198 *GERMANY: 1789*
ISAAC DANIEL ITZIG
Engraving
Rubens (ii) 2095
As a reformer he breaks away from tradition, wears contemporary dress with a toupee and side curls and is clean-shaven.

[23] Illustrations of both of these items of dress appear in Goldstein and Dresdner and there are actual examples in the Museum of Ethnography, Tel-Aviv.

195

196

197

198

200

199

199 *GERMANY: Eighteenth century*
[ARBA KANPHOTH AND PRAYER CAP]
Blue silk with gold embroidery
Musée de Cluny, Paris
Monumenta Judaica, *E 19.*

200 *GERMANY: Eighteenth century*
[BARRETTE]
Bayerisches Nationalmuseum, Munich
Round black felt hat worn by German Jews during the eighteenth century.
Monumenta Judaica *E 490.*

201 *GERMANY: Nuremberg 1755*
[JEWISH COSTUMES]
Engraving
From A. Wurfel, Historiche Nachrichten, *Nuremberg, 1755*
(From left to right):
1. The head of the congregation wears the mediaeval hood (kappe) *and a deep fringed collar. 2. Dress for synagogue. 3. Women's dress for synagogue includes the* viereckiger schleier *(square veil). 4. Synagogue dress. The head-dress seems to be the mediaeval* liripipe. *5. Women's indoor dress. 6. Carrying the Sabbath wine.*

Prospect der Juden Schul, wie sie stande, dort, wo jzt die Frauen Kirche.

Meridies

Oriens

Occidens

Septentriō.

ildnus eines Nürnber- ischen Juden Meisters, vie Er über die Gasse gegangen.

Ein Jud, wie Er zur Schule gegangen.

Ein Juden Weib, wie Sie zur Schul gegangen

n Jud wie Er außer er Schul gekleydet war.

Eine Jüdin in ihrer Haus kleydung.

Ein Jud, der Schabbas Wein abhohlet

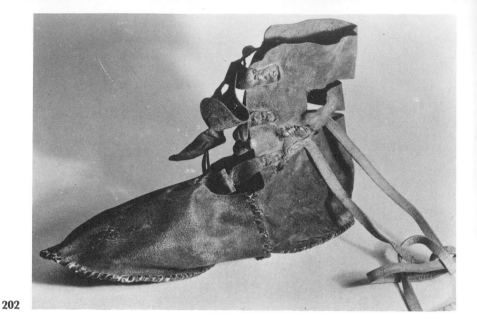

202

frill. The shoes are made without leather at the heels and everyone appears slipshod. Over their dress they wear a large silk gown (and in some instances even two) the sleeves of which hang down the back; a fur cloak is suspended from the neck . . . they take particular pride in their head dress of pearls; the more valuable denotes the distinction of wealth.'

The same writer has this to say of the men: 'The Lithuanian Jews are all dressed alike in long tunics of black silk with a broad silken sash round the waist; on the head they wear a small velvet cap and over it a huge one of fur'.[24]

Another traveller who stayed at a Jewish inn was struck by the curious cap decorated with pearls worn by the landlord's wife and learned that it was the mark of a married woman and was given as the bridal present by the husband.[25]

The Karaites of the Crimea were a Jewish sect with their own traditions and customs. They had their own village, Djufut-Kale, known as the fortress of the Jews because of its impregnable position, and they dressed like the other inhabitants of the region. All travellers who visited them are unanimous in praising their kindness, their civilised way of life and their high moral standards. An Englishman, who visited parts of Russia on

202 *AUSTRIA: Nineteenth century*
[CHALIZA SHOE]
Bezalel Jewish National Museum, Jerusalem
Formerly used by the Jewish community in Vienna.

203 *GERMANY: Seventeenth century*
[SIVLONOTH (MARRIAGE) BELTS]
1. Silver gilt; brocade on velvet and eleven rosettes of silver set with precious stones. Seventeenth century.
2. Silver; two strips of silver brocade; violet velvet. Dated 1693.
Bezalel Jewish National Museum, Jerusalem.

204 *GERMANY: Nineteenth century*
[BESCHNEIDUNGSMANTELCHEN: CIRCUMCISION COATS]
Silk and silver thread
Bezalel Jewish National Museum, Jerusalem
Monumenta Judaica E 110

205 *GERMANY: Eighteenth century*
[YOM KIPPUR BELT]
Brocade with silver clasp
Jewish Museum, London
Belt worn in synagogue on the Day of Atonement. The design follows a conventional form.

206 *GERMANY: Offenbach 1800*
[THE SEDER]
Engraving
From an Hagadah, Offenbach 1800
The master of the house and his sons still wear the flat round Jewish hat (barrette).

[24] Johnson, 376–8
[25] Macmichael, 44–7

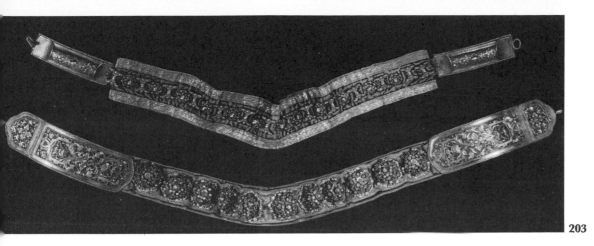

203

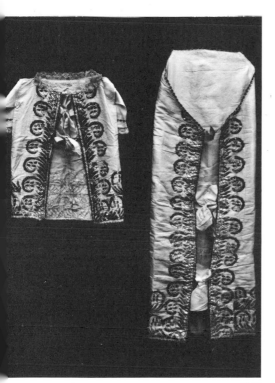

204

205

206

207

208

207 *GERMANY: Leipzig 1808*
[A POLISH JEW AND A GERMAN JEW]
Etching
From K. Lang, Die Hanshaltung der menschen, *Leipzig (1808)*
The Polish Jew in traditional dress; the German Jew in the costume of the previous century and bearded.

208 *GERMANY: c. 1820*
A HAMBURG JEWESS ON HER SABBATH
Drawing
Rubens (ii) 1636
She holds a pompadour parasol and wears very décolleté clothes under her synagogue cloak.

209 *GERMANY: c. 1800*
DER SAMSTAG
Engraving
Jewish Museum, London
The women are in Directoire dresses. The men have retained their traditional costume for synagogue: they have flat round hats (barrettes), *sleeveless gowns* (sarbals) *and frilled collars and wear beards.*

210 *SWITZERLAND: 1768*
[FUNERAL]
Engraving
From Ulrichs
The men are dressed like the German Jews in cloaks and round hats (barrettes).

209

210

211

behalf of the Bible Society, saw them in 1821 and attended the synagogue during Pentecost. He describes the Karaite *tallith* as consisting of two long belts of woollen material joined behind by a square piece of the same material ornamented in various ways and with *tsitsith* attached to its corners [see Plate 23]. The rabbi was dressed in a long robe of black silk over which a large white *tallith* was thrown covering his head. The ordinary people wore long blue top coats lined with lambskin and large lambskin caps.[26]

A Russian traveller, Prince Demidov, who visited the Karaites of Crimea in 1837, was impressed by the scrupulous care with which they dressed and their general air of distinction. An artist who accompanied him made a number of sketches [see Plates 163–5].

[26] Henderson, 325–6

211 *GERMANY: 1804*
ISRAEL JACOB
Engraving
Rubens (ii) 2096
A member of the reform group of German Jews in a bob-wig and the dress of the period.

212 *GERMANY: Frankfurt a/m 1866–9*
[WEDDING]
From Oppenheim
The bride and bridegroom both wear marriage belts of gold which, according to the text, were presents from one to the other. The rabbi in a tallith wears the Polish streimel. The other men wear three-cornered hats, knee-breeches and buckled shoes—the dress for synagogue and special occasions.

AUTHORITIES: A. N. Demidov; S. M. Dubnow; W. Eljasz; N. Gilyarovskaya; M. Goldstein & K. Dresdner; M. Grunwald; E. Henderson; L. Hollaenderski; *Jewish Encycl. s.v.* Russia and Poland; R. Johnson; W. Macmichael; Information concerning the *streimel* and the *spodic* from Professor B. Mark, Zydowski Instytut Historyazny, Warsaw; J. P. Norblin. See Bibliography.

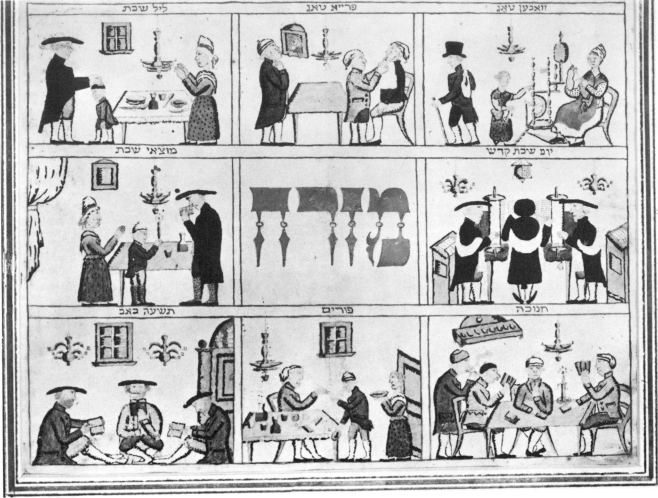

213

213 *GERMANY: c. 1820*
[MIZRACH]
Drawing
From the collection of Mr H. Eisemann
The day by day life of a Jew showing the traditional costume worn at home for prayers and the everyday clothes for work.

214–5 *DENMARK: c. 1800*
KLEIDERJUDE. BANDJUDE
Engravings
From G. L. Lahde, Kjobenhavns Klaededragter, *Copenhagen c. 1800*
They have the usual varied assortment of clothes worn by street vendors.

216 *AUSTRIA: Prague 1617*
[JEWS IN SYNAGOGUE]
Woodcut
From Shoshanat Haamakim, Prague 1617
They wear the flat berets (barrettes) *which had become a feature of Jewish costume.*

215

214

216

217

Western Europe

The revolution in men's and women's fashions in Europe during the sixteenth and seventeenth centuries is reflected in the Jewish Sumptuary Laws with their emphasis on austerity, their strict ban on novelties in dress and the rigid code which attempted to lay down the appropriate dress for every conceivable occasion.

The Christian Church also had its Sumptuary Laws, which were designed to curb luxurious living and, particularly, feminine extravagance. As early as the thirteenth century in Venice special magistrates, *Provveditori Sopra Le Pompe*, were appointed to enforce the regulations while in England, under Edward III, offenders were dealt with by Act of Parliament. In Italy during the eighteenth century the dress restrictions framed by the Church were almost as severe as those issued by the Synagogue authorities.[27]

Jewish restrictions on dress in times of trouble go back at least to the time of the Mishnah. According to Sotah ix:9: 'During the war of Vespasian the use of crowns by bridegrooms and the beating of the drums (at weddings) was forbidden. During the war of Titus the crowns of brides etc. were

217 *AUSTRIA: Prague c. 1650*
[BER TELLER]
Etching
From his Be'er Majjim Hajjim, *Prague c. 1650*
Statni Zidovske Museum, Prague
As a physician he is permitted by the communal regulations to wear the contemporary dress of his profession.

218 *AUSTRIA: 1710*
[JACOB RIES]
Engraving
Rubens (ii) 2189
Court jester at Vienna. As a Court Jew he wears contemporary dress and full-bottomed wig.

219 *AUSTRIA: Prague 1617*
[SYNAGOGUE INTERIOR]
Woodcut
From Shoshanat Haamakim, *Prague 1617*
The rabbi on the left wears a beret (barrette) with short-sleeved gown. The preacher on the right wears a hood and the congregation are in berets and cloaks.

[27] See M. Vaussard, *Daily Life in 18th century Italy*, London, 1962, 36 ff.

218

219

forbidden'. But the later Dress Regulations were designed mainly in order to resist Christian fashions and to avoid creating envy by extravagance and ostentation.

A Rabbinical Synod held at Frankfurt a/m in 1603 having noticed 'that many Jews wear clothing made after the manner of Gentiles and that many dress themselves and their daughters in costly clothes' decreed that such practices should cease.

Probably most Jewish communities had their Dress Regulations. Extracts from the laws of Forli in Italy (1416); Valladolid in Spain (1432); Metz (1690–4); Frankfurt-am-Main (1715); Hamburg (1715 and 1731) and Carpentras (1738) are given in the Appendix. In Italy the restrictions became much more severe after the sixteenth century.[28]

Most of them were aimed at women. All jewellery was severely restricted while *godrons* (a type of ruff) and the extravagant coiffures of the late seventeenth century (*en cheveux* and *fontanges*) were banned. At Metz veils of gold or silver were allowed on special occasions only and for some time *sivlonoth* belts were prohibited. Men's wigs were restricted to the size of clerical wigs. In Frankfurt women were obliged to wear hooded cloaks for synagogue and their shoes had to be black or white while men were not allowed coloured or white wigs. At Carpentras wigs with ribbons and curls and bagwigs *(perrukes à bourse)* were prohibited. In Hamburg women were not allowed crinolines. At Mantua at the end of the seventeenth century women were forbidden to use gold or silver embroidery and they were allowed very little jewellery. Outdoors they had to wear a long cloak with a hood covering the whole head. Only brides were allowed to wear gold and silver headbands with flowers. Men were not allowed to wear *sarbals* or other outer garments made of bright materials and bagwigs were forbidden. At Rome in 1726 men were forbidden to spend more than three escudos on their wigs.[29]

From the laws of Ancona in 1766 we learn that it was normal for men to wear the *arba kanphoth* in the street, this practice being forbidden in future except for bridegrooms on their wedding day. By the same laws hats with brims were prohibited for men but they were allowed to have a gold or lace border of a finger's width with a little tassel on their *berretta* while bridegrooms were permitted to

[28] Milano, 563–6
[29] *Pragmatica . . . Dall'Ebrei Di Roma,* Rome 1726. (Mocatta Library)

have it embroidered with silver or gold.[30]

At Modena in addition to the usual restrictions women were forbidden to wear trains to their dresses and they were not permitted to go into the town without a *cendale* (headdress) nor were they allowed to carry clocks, repeater watches or jewel cases uncovered. Men were forbidden to wear plumes, cockades or other ornaments in their hats.[31]

Wigs continued to receive rabbinical censure in Germany up to a late period. The communal physician's appointment at Fürth in 1760 was conditional on his abandoning his wig, and as late as 1781 Raphael Cohn of Altona [see Plate 275] excommunicated a Jew for wearing a bag-wig.

The Venetian rabbi, Leon of Modena (1571-1648), in his *Historia dei Riti Ebraici* written for James I of England emphasises the conservatism of Jewish dress. He writes:

'They do not willingly imitate any other Nation in the fashion of their apparell unless their own make them there seem very deformed. Neither may they shave their Crown, nor wear Locks of hair upon their head, nor any the like things. And in what country soever they are, they generally affect the long garment or gown. The women also apparell themselves in the habit of the countries where they inhabite. But when they are married, upon their Wedding Day they cover their own hair, wearing either a Perruke, or Dressing, or some other hair or something else that may counterfeit Natural Hair according to the Custome of the Women of that place, but they are never to appear in their own hair more . . . They hold it also an unbeseeming thing for a man to make himself ready without putting on a Girdle; or something that may divide the lower part of the body from the upper.'[32]

A Dutch writer gives this description of Jewish dress at the beginning of the eighteenth century:

'As the Men must not dress themselves like Women, so the Women are not allowed to disguise themselves in Men's Apparel. A Jew must avoid every Thing that may make him appear effeminate; Jewels, Pomatums, Paint, Patches, Spanish White &c., must be banished from the Toilet of the modest Jew, and left to the Fops and the Ladies; together with the Glass, and all the childish and affected Airs, which are the Consequences of consulting it. The faithful Jew must learn to be upon his Guard, to shew a great Soul, and with Patience suffer the fine black Locks he had at twenty-five to turn grey at forty-five. He must despise the Use of Nippers, or of any such Compositions as help to discolour the Beard,

[30] *Pragmatica . . . Degli Ebrei D'Ancona*, Ancona 1766. (Roth Collection)
[31] *Prammatica . . . Degli Ebrei Di Modena*, Modena 1790. (Author's collection)
[32] *The History of the Rites, Customs and Manner of Life of the Present Jews . . . translated into English by Edmund Chilmead*, London, 1650, 12-17.

220

221

220 *AUSTRIA: Prague 1734*
[PRAGUE. SYNAGOGUE SERVICE FOR NEW YEAR]
Engraving
Rubens (ii) 1157
Most of the men wear the prescribed dress for this occasion, the sargenes *or* kittel, *accompanied by the Jewish ruff.*

221 *AUSTRIA: c. 1690*
SAMUEL OPPENHEIMER
Engraving
Rubens (ii) 2179
As a Court Jew he is permitted to wear contemporary dress and a wig but he retains a beard and his dress is very simple.

222 *AUSTRIA: Prague 1741*
[PROCESSION OF JEWS OF PRAGUE ON THE BIRTH OF THE ARCHDUKE JOSEPH 24 APRIL 1741]
Engraving
Statni Zidovske Museum, Prague
A record of the remarkable variety of costumes worn by the Jews of Prague.

223 *AUSTRIA: Vienna c. 1800*
UN JUIF TURQUEOIS AVEC SA FAMILLE A VIENNE
Aquatint
Rubens (ii) 1887
They are in Turkish costume and the man does not wear the kaveze, *the typical head-dress of Turkish Jews. Many Turkish Jews took advantage of the Treaty of Passarowitz 1718, which permitted them to live in Vienna as Turkish subjects.*

223

224

smooth the wrinkles or fill up the holes in his face,
or to fasten in false teeth. This is the Duty incum-
bent on a devout Jew; but we will not say, that
all of them inviolably observe it. As there are
Laws and Rules relating to the Beard, it must
not wholly be omitted. The German Jews wear
their Beards from the Extremity of one Jaw to
the other, like a Cord, which is divided by a Tuft
into two equal Parts, which falls very agreeably
from the Chin upon the Breast.'[33]

Germany, Austria, Hungary and Switzerland shared very much the same customs as
regards Jewish dress. During the seventeenth
century the Jewish cloak, the *sarbal*, remained the distinctive outer garment and
Joseph Nördlingen Hahn (died 1637), in his
Sefer Yosef Ometz, exhorts Jews to wear one
when saying their prayers at home, instead
of the short house-jacket. The Sabbath *sarbal*
(*schülmantel*) was a cloak without an opening
on the right-hand side to remind the wearer
not to carry anything on the Sabbath day;
Hahn recalls that in his youth, when times
were better, most people had a *sarbal* exclu-
sively for synagogue use and the wealthy gave
one to their sons when they got married. He
attacked the modern practice of wearing a
sarbal with a vent at the back decorated with
multi-coloured silk, which made it an ornamental garment instead of a practical one.

224 *AUSTRIA: Vienna 1775*
TRODELJUD
Engraving
From Der Ausruf in Wien, 1775
*The pedlar is bearded and wears a coif in addition to the three-
cornered hat which he holds.*

225-6 *AUSTRIA: Prague c. 1760*
REICHER JUD IN PRAG
REICHE JÜDIN IN PRAG
Etchings
From the collection of Dr Arthur Polak
*The costumes are marked by their simplicity and subdued
colours. The woman has her hair partially covered and carries
a bonnet for outdoor wear.*

[33] Picart, 1733 ed. 246

225

226

227

228

229

227 *AUSTRIA: Prague 1806*
JONAS JEITTELES
Engraving
Rubens (ii) 2099
A physician, he wears bob wig and contemporary dress.

228 *AUSTRIA: Salzburg 1826*
[FEAST OF TABERNACLES]
Engraving
Title page to a Machsor, *Salzburg 1826*
The men in the traditional barrette, *Jewish ruff, knee breeches,*
tail coat and buckled shoes.

229 *AUSTRIA: 1804*
FANNY VON ARNSTEIN
Mezzotint
Rubens (ii) 2011
She wears the dress of fashionable Viennese Society in which
she figured prominently, and although married she has her
hair uncovered and in curls, for which she is said to have
incurred rabbinic censure.

230 *ITALY: Venice 1601*
[WEDDING]
Woodcut
From Minhagim, *Venice, 1601. Bodleian Library*
The men wear berets (the Jewish barrettes*) and cloaks: the*
women have kerchiefs attached to their bonnets.

231 *ITALY: Venice 1601*
[LIGHTING THE LIGHTS. EVE OF YOM KIPPUR]
Woodcut
From Minhagim, *Venice, 1601. Bodleian Library*
The mother of the family has her head covered and wears a
high collar.

230

231

232

Hahn also deplored the disappearance of the *matran*, formerly worn especially at Frankfurt-am-Main and Worms. This was the *chaperon*, the most characteristic feature of Jewish dress in mediaeval times, the great virtue of which, according to Hahn, was that it served to cover the head and eyes so that a person was completely enveloped during prayer, a practice which went back to Talmudic times.[34]

The *chaperon* had been replaced by the *barrette (beret)*, a round hat made of felt or wool, which was originally a symbol of learning popular all over Europe during the fifteenth and sixteenth centuries. For a long time it was the normal daily head-dress of the Jew but gradually became reserved for Synagogue use, hence the name, *schabbes deckel*, by which it was known to Jew and Christian alike. In its early form it had a loose floppy crown without any stiffening and the one example which has survived [Plate 200] is a late version which was still being worn during the nineteenth century [Plate 209].

An even more distinctive piece of costume for women as well as for men was the six-teenth-century ruff, the *Jüdenkragen*, which survived as a Jewish distinction either in its

232 *ITALY: Rome 1602*
HEBREA
Etching
British Museum
She wears a long robe and cloak and has a kerchief attached to her bonnet.

233 *ITALY: Venice 1710*
[MOSES CHEFEZ]
Engraving
Rubens (ii) 2039
A Hebrew scholar and teacher, he wears a coat buttoned to the neck and white bands. He is clean shaven and wears his own hair.

234 *ITALY: Venice 1719*
[ABRAHAM COHEN OF ZANTE]
Engraving
Rubens (ii) 2006
A physician, he wears full-bottomed wig and is clean shaven.

235 *ITALY: Reggio Nell'Emilia c. 1740*
[INTERIOR OF SYNAGOGUE]
Engraving
Rubens (ii) 1325
Most of the men wear three-cornered hats and tye-wigs and are clean shaven. A Levantine Jew is bearded and wears a turban.

[34] T. B. *Hagigah* 14B

233

הרופא הכהן מרדכי אברהם קאנפא ניל יצ"ו הפילוסוף הנאמן

234

235

236

237

236 *ITALY: Rome c. 1820*
[SERMON TO THE JEWS AT ROME]
Painting by Hieronymous Hess (1799–1850)
Copenhagen Museum
The annual conversionist sermon which the Jews of Rome were obliged to attend. A few Levantine Jews are bearded and wear turbans, the remainder are in contemporary dress.

237 *FRANCE: 1792*
[OLD CLOTHES DEALER]
Etching
Rubens (ii) 1572
In a three-cornered hat, wig and contemporary dress.

238 *ITALY: Reggio Nell'Emilia c. 1740*
[DEATH SCENE]
Engraving
Rubens (ii) 1326
The women in décolleté dresses, high coiffures and bonnets. Two bearded Levantine Jews in turbans are present; others are clean-shaven.

239 *FRANCE: 1664*
[JEW OF LORRAINE]
Etching
From S. Le Clerc, Divers estats et conditions de la vie humaine, *Paris 1664*
In a barrette and ruff as worn by the German Jews.

240 *ITALY: Florence 1806*
S. FIORENTINO
Engraving
From his Poesie, *Florence, 1806*
He is clean-shaven and wears a short wig with contemporary dress.

238

239

240

241

241 *FRANCE: 1806*
FURTADO DE LA GIRONDE
Engraving
Rubens (i) 101
A member of the Sephardi community of Bordeaux in a tye-wig
(à noeud) *and contemporary dress.*

242 *FRANCE: Nancy c. 1810*
[INTERIOR OF SYNAGOGUE AT NANCY]
Lithograph
Rubens (ii) 1576
*The rabbi, who is bearded, wears the traditional fur hat and
there are a few Levantine Jews in turbans; otherwise the dress
is contemporary and some of the men are in military uniform.*

243 *FRANCE: 1781*
[PASSPORT ISSUED BY BISHOP OF CARPENTRAS, 1781]
*Pursuant to Article 10 of the Decree of 18 July 1781 it grants
a Jew liberty to travel provided he wears a yellow hat if he
stays more than one day in any of the towns or villages of the
province.*

original form or as a pleated collar until well
into the nineteenth century. Another survival from mediaeval times was the *viereckiger
schleier* (square veil) worn by Jewish women
which was reserved for synagogue use and for
the Sabbath. It was a cap with two stiffly
starched pointed wings in front made of
white linen. It closely covered the head and
the bun of hair at the back and had two blue
stripes as a Jewish distinction [see Plates 190
and 201]. The normal everyday head-dress
for German women in the seventeenth century was a bonnet with cone-shaped ears.

For weddings the mothers of the bride and
bridegroom wore the mediaeval *fret*, a head-
dress made of gold or silver trellis-work
[Plates 184 and 192].

Maximilian Misson, who passed through
Frankfurt in November 1687, remarked on
the large number of Jews and was struck by
their pointed beards and black coats with
pleated ruffs.

Skippon, who also visited the Frankfurt
ghetto towards the end of the seventeenth
century, writes:

'Most of the men wear ruffs and the women are
habited with a black mantle; their head-dress is
of linen, which sticks out much on either side;
several of the women also wear ruffs. All the Jews

242

JOSEPH DE BENI,

Par la grace de Dieu & du de cette Ville de Carpentras, le PAPE, &c.

S. Siége Apostolique, Évêque Assistant au Trône de N. S. P.

EN conformité des Articles XXXVII. & XXXVIII. de l'Edit du 5 Avril 1775, & de l'Article X. du Décret de la Sacrée Congrégation du Saint Office du 18 Juillet 1781, Nous permettons à   Juif de la Carrière de cette Ville, d'aller en voyage soit dans cette Province du Comté Venaissin, soit dans les différentes Villes du Royaume de France, à condition que ledit

n'entreprendra point le susdit voyage avec un Conducteur Chrétien un jour de Dimanche ou Fête chaumée par les Chrétiens; qu'il ne pourra séjourner dans les Villes & Lieux du Diocèse de cette Ville où il n'y a point de Juiverie lesdits jours des Dimanches & Fêtes; & qu'en 243 conformité de l'Art. XX. dudit Edit, s'il s'arrête plus d'un jour dans les Villes ou Villages du Comtat, il sera tenu de porter le chapeau de couleur jaune. Les Présentes valables pour le terme de   à compter de ce jour. DONNÉ à Carpentras au Palais Episcopal, ce

244

244 *HOLLAND: 1668*
[CIRCUMCISION]
Painting by Romeyn de Hooghe
Rijksmuseum, Amsterdam
*The two rabbis are bearded and wear skull caps, knee breeches
and coats buttoned to neck. The other men with one exception
are clean shaven and wear wigs.*

245-6 *HOLLAND: 1723*
NUPTIAL CEREMONY OF THE PORTUGUESE JEWS
NUPTIAL CEREMONY OF THE GERMAN JEWS
Engravings
From Picart. Rubens (ii) 1239-40
*There is nothing unusual about the dress. The Sephardim
generally are clean-shaven and wear wigs while most of the
Ashkenazim have beards and their own hair. The Ashkenazi
bridegroom wears a wedding belt, and according to Picart he
sends the bride a marriage belt of gold the day before the wed-
ding while she sends him one of silver. On the wedding day the
bride has her head uncovered and her hair in tresses which in
Venice are curled and called* banetes.

245

246

247

wear a little yellow mark upon the clothes for distinction.'[35]

Edmund Chishull, who travelled through Austria in 1698, visited one of the eight synagogues at Prague and found the Jews wearing a blue ruff as a mark of distinction.

The Jewish Badge makes its final appearance in Germany in an unusual heart-shaped form on an engraving published at the beginning of the eighteenth century [Plate 180]. It was no longer being worn at Frankfurt-Am-Main in 1714 according to Schudt, who observes that the Jews everywhere were discarding their distinctive clothing although this was not a sign of their approaching conversion but more of their growing pride and insolence.

'Now,' he says, 'the Jews wear black coats, black hats and dark-coloured clothes with a turnover of linen round the neck. The older and nobler ones often wear a round white pleated collar . . . On the Sabbath the married men wear this collar with a flat round beret of black cloth which has no iron ring inside and hangs down from his head. Our people call it Schabbes Deckel. . . . The older men go fully adorned to the Synagogue wearing silk jackets and coats of costly material; some even have fine wigs. They also wear slippers so as not to appear to be hurrying away from a holy place but to be dressed for peace and quiet as if they were at home. . . . In Frankfurt the women wore up to the last fire in 1711 pointed

247 *HOLLAND: 1642*
ZACUTUS LUSITANUS
Engraving
Rubens (ii) 2241
The famous physician is bearded and wears a deep collar edged with lace and a cuff to match.

248 *HOLLAND: 1780*
[PURIM. MASKED BALL]
Etching
Rubens (ii) 1359

249 *HOLLAND: c. 1685*
[FRANCISCO LOPES SUASSO]
Painting
Stedelijk Museum, Amsterdam
He is clean shaven, has a full-bottomed wig and is dressed in the extravagant costume of the period.

250 *ENGLAND: 1721*
[DR FERNANDO MENDEZ]
Miniature by Catherine da Costa
Spanish and Portuguese Synagogue, Bevis Marks, London.
In full-bottomed wig, contemporary dress and doctor's gown.

[35] Skippon, 442

248

249

250

251

252

251 *ENGLAND: c. 1740*
[MOSES HART]
Oil painting
Great Synagogue, London
A leader of the London Ashkenazim, in full-bottomed powdered wig and contemporary dress.

252 *ENGLAND: c. 1788*
[LORD GEORGE GORDON]
Mezzotint
Rubens (i) 139
In the dress he adopted after his conversion to Judaism; long beard and the large felt hat worn by Polish Jews.

253 *ENGLAND: 1749*
THE JERUSALEM INFIRMARY
Engraving
Rubens (i) 295
The chief figures in this caricature represent prominent members of the English Sephardi community and the medical staff of the Infirmary. All are clean-shaven and wear contemporary dress but various types of wig are shown. The caricaturist evidently regards as affectations the bag-wig of the man at the table and the divided or Campaign wig of the physician, Jacob de Castro Sarmento, (standing behind the monkey), as well as the sword which he alone carries.

254 *ENGLAND: 1780*
[RAPHAEL FRANCO]
Oil painting by Thos. Gainsborough
Member of a leading Sephardi family in a yellow coat, vest and breeches, lace stock and frills and a tye-wig.

253

254

255

stiff veils with a blue stripe. These have now fallen into disuse like the yellow rings of the men. When I visited three women's Schuls on the eve of Schabbes in October 1713 I found among several hundred Jewish women only one wearing such a veil. All the others wore bonnets with a wide lace border. When I enquired the reason I was told that all the veils were burned in the great fire . . . . Round the neck they had large round collars like the men's but theirs were starched stiffly. Over their clothes they wore wide black cloaks. Widows cover their heads with a piece of white linen which hangs down the back. . . . The women are gradually discarding the coats and collars and wear instead large, often precious lace kerchiefs. Many wear gold tinsel, gold lace or other precious ornaments on their heads especially unmarried women. Usually they have a silver belt round their waist. On Schabbes and feast days one sees with surprise what precious materials silks and laces are worn by the women folk.'[36]

The Sephardim of Hamburg, like their brethren in Amsterdam and London, wore wigs and the latest fashions in dress, much to the indignation of Schudt who notes that the unmarried women there wore such precious and fashionable clothes that they could not be distinguished from Christians. In Plate 179 they are seen wearing *fontanges*. During the eighteenth century the Hamburg Senate forbade Jews to appear on the Bourse with walking sticks, swords and pistols

255 *ENGLAND: 1799*
DAVID LEVI
Engraving
Rubens (i) 162
Although an orthodox Ashkenazi he wears a short bob powdered wig, is clean-shaven and his dress conforms to current fashions.

256 *ENGLAND: 1797*
[THE MONTEFIORE FAMILY]
Pastel
Formerly owned by the late Mr Julian Q. Henriques.
Joseph Elias Montefiore in a short wig, tail coat and knee breeches; his wife, Rachel, also apparently in a wig and a remarkable hat.

257 *ENGLAND: 1788*
THE ROYAL EXCHANGE. *(London)*
Engraving (detail)
A figure in a long cloak is seen on the right. His beard and outlandish dress identify him as a foreign-born Ashkenazi Jew.

258 *ENGLAND: 1806*
ABRM GOLDSMID ESQ.
Etching
Rubens (i) 118
Powdered tye-wig, frock, frilled shirt, high boots and knee breeches.

[36] Schudt ii: 241 ff. The author generally is completely unreliable but presumably in the case of Frankfurt he spoke from personal knowledge.

256

257

258

260

259

261

262

259 *ENGLAND: c. 1820*
[RACHEL DE CRASTO]
Oil painting
National Trust
Member of a leading Sephardi family in dress of the period.

260 *ENGLAND: 1815*
JOSHUA VAN OVEN
Engraving
Rubens (i) 288
Physician and a leading Ashkenazi. He is clean-shaven, wears his own hair and is dressed according to current fashion.

261 *ENGLAND: c. 1820*
OLD CLOTHES TO SELL
Etching
Rubens (ii) 1516
Jewish old-clothesman in typical costume with a tier of hats on his head as the sign of his trade.

262 *AMERICA: New York c. 1750*
[JACOB FRANKS]
Painting
From H. R. London, Portraits of Jews, *New York, 1927*
Prominent New York Ashkenazi wearing a divided wig, cravat and velvet coat of the period.

263 *AMERICA: c. 1750*
[PHILA FRANKS]
Painting
From H. R. London, Portraits of Jews, *New York, 1927.*
She wears the dress of the period.

N

263

264

'thereby causing disturbances and envy'.

Ulrichs, a sympathetic and reliable observer, who in 1768 published a history of Swiss Jewry, could find little in the city archives at Zurich on the subject of Jewish dress apart from an order issued by Bishop Hugo in 1497 requiring Swiss Jews to wear a yellow badge and women to have two blue stripes on their veils.

'Nowadays,' Ulrichs writes 'the Jews in Germany wear black cloaks, black hats and clothes commonly of dark colours. I do not remember ever to have seen a Jew in scarlet, green or sky blue or similar colours but I saw many dressed in black damask. The women however display much finery. They wear precious rings and beautiful dresses embroidered with gold and silver. The rabbis and Parnassim, the teachers and heads of the Jewish community, also the older and highly esteemed persons wear a round white linen collar with many pleats.'[37]

The tendency noted by Schudt for German Jews to drop their distinctive costume becomes increasingly noticeable as the eighteenth century progresses. Physicians and Court Jews wore wigs and contemporary dress as did men of letters and the old dress regulations were no longer enforced, but it was not until 1781 that the Emperor Joseph II abolished all distinctions in Bohemia including the yellow cuffs of the Jews of Prague

264 *ENGLAND: c. 1840*
BARON LIONEL DE ROTHSCHILD
Lithograph
Rubens (i) 231
In top hat and frock with fashionable side-whiskers.

265 *ASHKENAZI RABBINICAL DRESS
HOLLAND: 1700*
[JEHIEL MICHAEL]
Engraving
Rubens (ii) 2148
Rounded unkempt beard, broad-brimmed hat and full length clerical robes with white bands.

266 *AMERICA: Philadelphia c. 1775*
[MICHAEL PRAGER]
Oil painting by Jas. Peale
The Insurance Company of North America
He wears a wig with a pigtail queue, frock, waistcoat and frilled shirt.

267 *ASHKENAZI RABBINICAL DRESS
GERMANY: Eighteenth century*
[RABBI FROM GELNHAUSEN]
Painting
Jüdisches Lexikon IV (1), 1202
In a barrette, *pleated collar and fur-trimmed coat.*

[37] Ulrichs, 49–53

266

265

267

268

269

268 *ASHKENAZI RABBINICAL DRESS*
GERMANY: 1762
HIRSCH MICHAEL
Etching
Rubens (ii) 2146
Full beard, traditional fur hat (spodic) and fur-trimmed robe
with girdle.

269 *ASHKENAZI RABBINICAL DRESS*
AUSTRIA: Prague 1773
DAVID BEN ABRAHAM OPPENHEIMER
Engraving
Rubens (ii) 2162
Wearing traditional fur-trimmed hat (spodic) and an em-
broidered coat with frogs on the shoulders and down the front.

270 *ASHKENAZI RABBINICAL DRESS*
HOLLAND: c. 1770
[EMANUEL COHEN]
Drawing
Rubens (ii) 2040
With unkempt beard, traditional fur hat (spodic) and
voluminous gown.

270

271

272

271 *ASHKENAZI RABBINICAL DRESS*
HOLLAND: 1793
[JACOB LOWENSTAM]
Engraving
Rubens (ii) 2122
In the traditional dress of the Polish rabbi: fur-trimmed hat
(spodic), *long gown and girdle.*

272 *ASHKENAZI RABBINICAL DRESS*
AUSTRIA: Prague c. 1790
[EZEKIEL LANDAU]
Engraving
Rubens (ii) 2103
Wearing the traditional rabbinical hat, the spodic.

273 *ASHKENAZI RABBINICAL DRESS*
ENGLAND: 1779
REV. ISAAC POLACK
Mezzotint
Rubens (i) 224
He is clean-shaven and wears a three-cornered hat, clerical
robes with white bands and a short bob powdered wig.

273

274

and the yellow stripes worn by unmarried Jewish women.

Closer social contacts between Jews and Christians also had their effect and Fanny von Arnstein [Plate 229] is said to have shocked Viennese Jewish opinion by wearing her hair uncovered, although she had been forestalled in this respect by Blumchen Friedlander [Plate 197] at Berlin.

The traditional Jewish costume of the seventeenth and eighteenth centuries was retained in Germany for the Sabbath and is seen in a striking picture of the late eighteenth century [Plate 209]. This costume gradually fell into disuse and a new tradition—a three-cornered hat, knee breeches and buckled shoes—is seen in the Oppenheim pictures of the 1860's showing Jewish life in Frankfurt-am-Main [Plate 212]. A somewhat similar costume but with the customary Jewish barrette is found at Salzburg in 1826 [Plate 228], which again follows very closely the description of the communal dress of the Jews of Mattersdorf in Hungary at the middle of the nineteenth century. This, we are told, comprised shoes with silver buckles, white or black silk socks, velvet knee breeches with silver buckles, a coloured waistcoat and a tail coat both with silver

274 *ASHKENAZI RABBINICAL DRESS*
GERMANY: 1798
HIRSCHEL LOEBEL
Engraving
Rubens (i) 173
In the typical dress of a German rabbi: fur hat (spodic) *and fur-trimmed robe.*

275 *ASHKENAZI RABBINICAL DRESS*
GERMANY: 1798
RAPHAEL COHN
Mezzotint
Rubens (ii) 2188
In traditional fur hat (spodic) *and fur-trimmed robe.*

276 *ASHKENAZI RABBINICAL DRESS*
AUSTRIA: Moravia c. 1800
[MOSES NIKOLSBERG]
Engraving
Rubens (ii) 2156
He has a long trimmed beard and wears a three-cornered hat.

277 *ASHKENAZI RABBINICAL DRESS*
FRANCE: c. 1806
[JOSEPH DAVID SINTZHEIM]
Engraving
Rubens (ii) 2222
The French Chief Rabbi is heavily bearded and wears a fur-trimmed hat of an unusual shape with clerical robes and white bands.

278 *ASHKENAZI RABBINICAL DRESS*
ENGLAND: c. 1805
SOLOMON HIRSCHEL
Engraving
Rubens (i) 149
The English Chief Rabbi in traditional fur hat and a robe with clerical bands. Probably his Sabbath dress.

זאת צורת הרב מהורר
ירפאל כהן,
יֹאבֵד ורֹם רֹשֹק אֹהֹ,
יֹתֹקֹנֹט לֹי,

275

276

277

278

279

buttons, a Maria-Stuart collar called *krais* and a green cloak fastened in front by a silver clasp called *schülmantel*. This last was also worn in the house for prayers and seems to have been a survival of the *sarbal*. A skull cap was worn under a *barette* without which no one could be called to the Law. The rabbi at Mattersdorf wore a *streimel* on the Sabbath and a boat-shaped hat on other days. Learned men wore a long coat trimmed with fur called a *power* but were clean-shaven, and the custom of wearing a full beard came later after Simon Schreiber became Rabbi at Mattersdorf in 1842.[38]

The Jewish woman seen on an etching published in Rome in 1602 [Plate 232] wears a bonnet with a kerchief attached which may have been yellow in colour as a mark of distinction. The woodcuts in the early seventeenth century *Minhagim* book [Plates 230–1] and *Hagadah* published in Venice show the men wearing berets and sarbals in synagogue while the women at home are in attractive contemporary costume. This is in keeping with the comments of the English traveller, Thomas Coyat, who visited the synagogue at Venice in June 1608 and saw in the gallery 'many Jewish women, whereof some were as beautiful as ever I saw, and so

279 *ASHKENAZI RABBINICAL DRESS GERMANY: 1808*
ARON BEER
Mezzotint
Rubens (ii) 2014
He has only a very slight beard and wears a gown with clerical bands and a three-cornered hat.

280 *ASHKENAZI RABBINICAL DRESS ENGLAND: 1808*
SOLOMON HIRSCHEL
Engraving
Rubens (i) 148
In three-cornered hat with clerical robes and white bands. Probably his everyday dress.

281 *ASHKENAZI RABBINICAL DRESS FRANCE: c. 1820*
JACOB MEYER
Lithograph
Rubens (ii) 2143
In a full beard and wearing a three-cornered hat with clerical robes and white bands.

282 *ASHKENAZI RABBINICAL DRESS HOLLAND: 1813*
SAMUEL BERENSTEIN
Engraving
Rubens (ii) 2022
The Amsterdam Chief Rabbi wears a three-cornered hat, beard, clerical gown, broad silk girdle and white bands.

[38] M. Grunwald, *Mattersdorf* in *Jahrbuch für jüdische Volkskunde*, Berlin–Wien 1925 ii: 477–8

280

281

282

284

283

285

283 *ASHKENAZI RABBINICAL DRESS*
FRANCE: c. 1823
NAPHTALI LAZAR HIRSCH
Lithograph
Rubens (ii) 2087
In a full beard and round fur hat.

284 *ASHKENAZI RABBINICAL DRESS*
HOLLAND: Amsterdam 1809
[ARYEH JUDAH KALISCH]
Engraving
Rubens (ii) 2101
In a fur-trimmed hat, frilled collar and ornamental cuffs.

285 *ASHKENAZI RABBINICAL DRESS*
HUNGARY: Presburg c. 1830
MOSES SCHREIBER
Lithograph
Rubens (ii) 2200
Heavily bearded, in a fur-trimmed hat (spodic) and fur-trimmed robe.

286 *ASHKENAZI RABBINICAL DRESS*
FRANCE: 1826
SIMON CAHN
Lithograph
Rubens (ii) 2034
In a trimmed beard and wearing a three-cornered hat with clerical robe and bands.

287 *ASHKENAZI RABBINICAL DRESS*
ENGLAND: 1827
REV. MYER LEVY
Lithograph
Rubens (i) 166
He is clean-shaven and wears a three-cornered hat which by this time was completely out of fashion.

286

287

288

gorgeous in their apparel, jewels, chains of gold, and rings adorned with precious stones, that some of our English countesses do scarce exceede them, having marvailous long traines like Princesses that are borne up by waiting women serving for the same purpose'.

When Misson visited Venice in 1688 the men were wearing red hats lined and trimmed with black but at Leghorn, which was a Free Port, the Jews were not required to wear any distinctive marks.

Jewish costume was less inhibited in Italy than anywhere else on the Continent except for Holland. Venice was the birthplace of David Nieto, the first English Haham to wear a wig [Plate 294] and the freedom enjoyed there is demonstrated by the early eighteenth century portraits of Moses Chefez in academical dress and Abraham Cohen of Zante in full-bottomed wig [Plates 233–4).

At Reggio Nell 'Emilia the women wore décolleté dresses and the men in synagogue had three-cornered hats and tye-wigs [Plates 235–8]. By contrast, in the Papal States, which included the Comtat Venaissin, the Jews were required to wear a yellow hat up to the time of the French Revolution.

In Alsace and Lorraine [Plate 239] the Jews probably followed the dress customs of

288 *ASHKENAZI RABBINICAL DRESS*
AUSTRIA: Prague c. 1830
[SAMUEL LANDAU]
Lithograph
Rubens (i) 2104
In a high fur hat (spodic) *and full beard.*

289 *ASHKENAZI RABBINICAL DRESS*
GERMANY: Oldenburg c. 1835
SAMSON RAPHAEL HIRSCH
Lithograph
Formerly in the possession of Mr H. Eiseman
The leader of German orthodox Jewry has a short trimmed beard and wears clerical robes with white bands. No hat is visible.

290 *ASHKENAZI RABBINICAL DRESS*
FRANCE: 1850
LE RABBIN
Engraving
Rubens (ii) 1578
Full beard; three-cornered hat, clerical robes and long white bands.

291 *ASHKENAZI RABBINICAL DRESS*
HOLLAND: c. 1840
J. L. LOWENSTAM
Lithograph
Rubens (ii) 2121
In a three-cornered hat and clerical bands; short beard.

289

290

291

292

293

292 *SEPHARDI RABBINICAL DRESS*
HOLLAND: 1686
YSHACK ABOAB
Mezzotint
Rubens (ii) 2004
With full beard and wearing a skull cap, plain white collar
and clerical gown.

293 *SEPHARDI RABBINICAL DRESS*
HOLLAND: c. 1650
JACOB YEHUDAH LEON TEMPLO
Engraving
Rubens (i) 158
His collar has a lace border; otherwise the skull cap and gown
form the usual dress of a Sephardi rabbi. His moustache and
stiletto beard are in keeping with current fashion.

294 *SEPHARDI RABBINICAL DRESS*
ENGLAND: 1705
DAVID NIETO
Engraving
Rubens (i) 218
The English Haham is bareheaded and has a stiletto beard.
He wears a full-bottomed wig and clerical robes with white
bands. His dress is an expression of his independent and liberal
outlook.

294

295

295 *ASHKENAZI RABBINICAL DRESS*
ENGLAND: 1904
THE CHIEF RABBI
From Vanity Fair, *31 March 1904*
Rubens (i) 391
Herman Adler in clerical robes, white bands and round hat,
the dress introduced from Hanover by his father and as worn
at the present time by the English Chief Rabbi.

296 *SEPHARDI RABBINICAL DRESS*
PALESTINE: c. 1690
[HEZEKIAH DA SILVA]
Lithograph (from a seventeenth century drawing)
Mocatta Library
He wears a kaveze, *the traditional head-dress of Turkish*
Jews, and a fur-trimmed pelisse.

296

297

German Jewry.

The Sephardim of Bordeaux wore wigs and contemporary dress [Plate 241].

No restrictions on Jewish dress existed in Holland and the Sephardim wore the latest fashions including wigs. Their women appeared in *fontanges* when this head-dress was introduced in the seventeenth century.[39]

The first Jews to return to England in the seventeenth century were Sephardim. They were indistinguishable from Englishmen in their dress; they had neat pointed Spanish beards and wigs. John Greenhalgh, described them after a visit to their synagogue in 1662 as 'all gentlemen and most of them rich in apparel, divers with jewels glittering . . . several of them are comely, gallant, proper gentlemen'.[40] The Ashkenazim could usually be recognized by their ragged beards and foreign dress but by the end of the eighteenth century even the more orthodox of the English born like David Levi [Plate 255] had discarded their beards and had adopted wigs and contemporary clothing. New immigrants tended to retain their native mode of dress and the beard remained a Jewish mark of distinction until it came into general fashion towards the middle of the nineteenth century. The 'ol-clo' man

297 *SEPHARDI RABBINICAL DRESS HOLLAND: 1728*
SALOMON AELYON
Engraving
Rubens (i) 13
Without a hat, in a full-bottomed wig, square-cut beard and gown with white border and clerical bands.

298 *SEPHARDI RABBINICAL DRESS ITALY: 1735*
[MENACHEM VIVANTE OF CORFU AGED 85]
Painting
Jewish Museum, London
In skull cap, full beard, clerical robes and girdle.

299 *SEPHARDI RABBINICAL DRESS ENGLAND: 1751*
MOSES GOMES DE MESQUITA
Mezzotint
Rubens (i) 210
The English Haham has a bush beard and wears a three-cornered hat, full-bottomed wig and clerical robes with white bands.

300 *SEPHARDI RABBINICAL DRESS ENGLAND: 1790*
REV. DAVID DE CRASTO
Engraving
Rubens (i) 72
He is clean-shaven and wears clerical robes with white bands and a physical wig.

[39] Rubens, *Iconography* Pl. 1008   [40] Hyamson, 19

1735
EcceL. Menachem
Viuante Rabinue
Vniuersitatis Heb
reorum Corcyre
Anno Etatis Sue
LXXXV.   298

299

300

o

301 *SEPHARDI RABBINICAL DRESS
HOLLAND: 1797*
DANIEL COHEN D'AZEVEDO

301

Engraving. Rubens (ii) 2012
*He has a full beard and wears a three-cornered hat, wig and
clerical bands.*

wearing a tier of hats as a sign of his calling
was always a Jew [Plate 261]. Sephardi and
Ashkenazi women dressed according to the
fashions of the day but it was usual for married women to keep their heads covered.

Rabbinical dress

There is no traditional rabbinical dress and
the robes worn at the present time are
derived from the black Geneva gown and
white bands of the Calvinist or Reformed
Church, while the round black hat which
was adopted in Austria and Germany during
the nineteenth century must be derived ultimately from the similar headgear of the
Greek Orthodox clergy.

Only in a few cases can one find any
marked distinction between rabbinical and
lay dress prior to the seventeenth century.
In the Holkham Bible Zachariah wears a
rather unusual collar which perhaps denoted
a priest [Plate 123] and the Portuguese rabbi
[Plate 144] wears a tall cylindrical hat with
a black gown but is clean-shaven. Ashkenazi
rabbinical dress developed gradually. The
Prague rabbi seen in a woodcut dating from
1617 has a distinctive gown [Plate 219] and
the preacher in Plate 177 has unusually wide
sleeves. The rabbi at Fürth [Plate 183] wears

302 *SEPHARDI RABBINICAL DRESS
AMERICA: 1772*
[HAIM ISAAC CARIGAL]
Painting. Yale University Library
*The following description of the rabbi's dress was recorded by
Ezra Stiles:*

'*Common English Shoes, black Leather, Silver flowered
Buckles, White Stockings. His general Habit was Turkish.
A green Silk Vest or long under garment reaching down more
than half way the Legs or within 3 Inches of the Ankles, the
ends of the Sleeves of this Vest appeared on the Wrists in a
foliage Turn-up of 3 inches, & the Opening little larger than
that the hand might pass freely. A Girdle or Sash of different
Colors red and green girt the Vest around his Body. It appeared
not to be open at the bottom but to come down like a petticoat;
and no Breeches could be discovered. This Vest however had an
opening above the Girdle—and he put in his Handkerchief,
and Snuff-box, and Watch. Under this was an inner Vest of
Calico, besides other Jewish Talismans. Upon the vest first
mentioned was a scarlet outer Garment of Cloth, one side
of it was Blue, the outside scarlet; it reached down about an
Inch lower than the Vest, or near the Ankles. It was open before,
no range of Buttons &c. along the Edge, but like a Scholars
Gown in the Body but plain and without many gatherings at
the Neck, the sleeves strait or narrow and slit open 4 or 5 Inches
at the End, and turned up with a blue silk Quarter Cuff,
higher up than at the End of the sleeve of the Vest. When he
came into the Synogogue he put over all, the usual Alb or white
Surplice, which was like that of other Jews, except that its
Edge was striped with Blue Straiks, and had more Fringe.
He had a White Cravat round his Neck. He had a long black
Beard, the upper Lip partly shaven—his Head shaved all over.
On his Head a high Fur (Sable) Cap, exactly like a Woman's
Muff, and about 9 or 10 Inches high, the Aperture atop was
closed with green cloth. He behaved modestly and reverently.'*
*(L. M. Friedman, Rabbi Haim Isaac Carigal, Boston,
1940, 4–5.)*

303

a plain white collar instead of a ruff. At Nuremberg the rabbi is shown wearing a *chaperon* as late as 1755 [Plate 201] but by this period a fairly general custom had grown up for Ashkenazi rabbis to wear a fur-trimmed Polish hat *(spodic)* with a fur-trimmed robe. In Austria, Hungary and East Germany an embroidered coat, Polish in origin, with frogs down the centre and on the shoulders was worn [Plate 269]. By the end of the eighteenth century the three-cornered hat was tolerated just about the time it was going out of fashion and it survived until the latter part of the nineteenth century. In England, Solomon Hirschel, the Chief Rabbi [Plates 278–80] wore one for weekdays but for Sabbath retained the fur hat worn by his father, Hart Lyon [Plate 274]. In the Oppenheim pictures [Plate 212] the rabbi with a *streimel* presumably came from Galicia. Most Ashkenazi rabbis wore beards and did not tolerate wigs.

A new style for rabbinic dress was introduced into England from Hanover by Nathan Marcus Adler when he was appointed Chief Rabbi in 1845. His son, who succeeded him, is said to have worn bishop's gaiters and his dress as seen in Plate 295

303 *SEPHARDI RABBINICAL DRESS*
ITALY: Turin c. 1806
ABRAHAM DE COLOGNA
Engraving
Rubens (ii) 2007
Bareheaded, clean-shaven and wearing clerical bands.

304 *SEPHARDI RABBINICAL DRESS*
ENGLAND: 1806
RAPHAEL MELDOLA
Engraving
Rubens (i) 180
The English Haham is clean-shaven and wears a three-cornered hat, long bob powdered wig, clerical robes and bands.

305 *SEPHARDI RABBINICAL DRESS*
HOLLAND: 1824
DAVID LEON
Engraving
Rubens (ii) 211
Clean-shaven and wearing three-cornered hat, bob wig and clerical bands.

306 *REFORM RABBINICAL DRESS*
GERMANY: Hamburg 1843–7
[NAPHTALI FRANKFURTER]
Lithograph
Rubens (ii) 1637
The reform rabbi is clean-shaven and wears a skull cap with a pompon, clerical bands, full length black gown and tallith.

304

305

306

betrays more than a suspicion of Anglican influence.

Western Sephardi rabbis had adopted conventional clerical dress long before then. In the seventeenth century the Dutch Sephardi rabbis wore a black coat buttoned to the neck with a white collar, knee breeches and a large sombrero type of hat [Plate 245]; otherwise they are usually seen in a skull cap [Plate 244] but both this and their stiletto or Vandyke beards were in keeping with current fashion and usually there was no fetish about keeping the head continuously covered as there was with the Ashkenazim. In England, Moses Cohen d'Azevedo, appointed Haham in 1761, was clean shaven and wore a powdered physical wig without a hat,[41] in these respects being followed precisely by his Hazan, David de Crasto [Plate 300]. Already in 1705, Haham David Nieto [Plate 294] was wearing a full-bottomed wig without a hat and a clerical robe with bands.

The rabbi of the Reform congregation at Hamburg wears a round cap with a pompon, black gown and bands [Plate 306].

Italian rabbis were usually clean-shaven and wore clerical robes with white bands [Plate 303]. They had no objection to wigs.

[41] Hyamson Pl. facing p. 113

In France the rabbis followed the customs of the Ashkenazim of Germany and Holland [Plate 277 etc.].

AUTHORITIES: I. Abrahams; J. A. Boener; A. Cahen; T. Coryat; A. Danon; M. Davenport; *Encyc. Judaica*; L. Finkelstein; H. Graetz; M. Grunwald; J. N. Hahn; J. A. Hammerton; M. Harrison; F. Hottenroth; *Jewish Encycl.*; *Jüdisches Lexikon*; B. Kisch; G. Kisch; *Monumenta Judaica*; M. Oppenheim; J. K. Schudt; S. Stern; J. C. Ulrichs; *Universal Jewish Encycl. See Bibliography*.

Appendix

EXTRACTS FROM JEWISH SUMPTUARY LAWS
AND DRESS REGULATIONS

Extracts from Laws made by a Commission held in 1416 at Forli in Italy:[1]

In order that we may carry ourselves modestly and humbly before the Lord, our God, and to avoid arousing the envy of the Gentiles, we decree that until the end of the above-mentioned term (ten years, 1416–26) no Jew or Jewess shall be permitted to make a *foderato-cinto*, unless it be black, and that the sleeves shall be open and that the sleeves shall have no silk lining whatever on them. Those who already possess such cloaks (*foderato-cinto*) of any colour other than black, may continue to wear them, provided the sleeves are not open, and the cloaks are closed both in the front and back.

Neither shall any man or woman wear any cloak of sable or ermine or mixed fur or of red material of mixed colour or of muslin or of violet colour. However, a cloak lined with fur may be worn, if none of the fur is placed on the outer covering of the cloak.

Women's cloaks which have already been made with open sleeves and are lined with fur, may be worn within the house but not in public, unless the sleeves are sewn or the cloaks are worn under an overcoat, so that the cloak cannot be seen at all. Also the coats of women which are lined with fur, must so far as possible be so made so as not to show the fur.

No man shall be permitted to wear a silk or velvet *giubetta* (cloak) except in such manner that it is completely concealed. Neither shall women wear any silk or velvet dress except in such manner that it is completely concealed. Neither shall they wear any dress having fringes attached to it other than at the opening of the neck or the sleeves.

No woman shall wear any necklace on her neck or a gold hair-net on her head unless it be concealed except that newly-married brides may wear golden hair-nets unconcealed for thirty days after the wedding; after that time they must wear the veil over the net. No girdle which has a silver buckle more than six ounces in weight, or which is covered with velvet in any form, shall be worn by men in public.

No more than one gold ring may be worn by a man, but the ring may be placed on any finger. Women shall under no circumstances wear more than two or three rings.

Neither shall women wear a girdle or belt the silver of which weighs more than ten ounces.

The fine for the transgression of any of these provisions regarding the use of clothes and ornaments shall be ten Bolognini of silver or their value for the treasury of the city for each offence. Men shall be held responsible for the infractions of these rules by their wives. If anyone will refuse to obey the ordinances, the community shall refuse to admit him to *minyan* or to read the Torah or to perform the *Gelilah*.

We have also decreed that it shall be prohibited for more than three ladies and two maids to walk together in the streets except in the performance of some religious duty. Nor shall it be permitted for women to promenade through the streets and avenues except on festival days, when they shall be limited in the said manner. Men shall be held responsible for the observance of this section by their wives as in the case of the dresses.

Extracts from Laws made by a Synod of Castilian Jews convened at Valladolid in 1432[2]

No woman unless unmarried or a bride in the first year of her marriage, shall wear costly dresses of gold-cloth, or olive coloured material or fine linen or silk, or of fine wool. Neither shall they wear on their dresses trimmings of velvet or brocade or olive-coloured cloth. Nor shall they wear a golden brooch nor one of pearls, nor a string of pearls on the forehead, nor dresses with trails on the ground more than one third of a *vara* in measure, nor fringed Moorish garments, nor coats with high collars, nor cloth of a high reddish colour, nor a skirt of *bermeia* thread, except as for the skirt and stockings, nor shall they make wide sleeves on the Moorish garments of more than two palms in width, but they may wear jewellery like silver brooches and silver belts provided that there is not more than four ounces of silver on any of them.

[1] Finkelstein, 292–3   [2] Finkelstein, 373–4

No son of Israel of the age of fifteen or more shall wear any cloak of gold-thread, olive-coloured material or silk, or any cloak trimmed with gold or olive-coloured material or silk, nor a cloak with rich trimmings nor with trimmings of olive-coloured or gold cloth.

This prohibition does not include the clothes worn at a time of festivity or at the reception of a lord or a lady, nor at balls or similar social occasions.

Because of the diversity of custom among the Communities in regard to the wearing apparel, we find it impracticable to make a general ordinance which shall provide for all the details that ought to be included, and we therefore ordain that each Community shall make such ordinances on the subject so long as this Ordinance endures, as will keep before their minds that we are in Dispersion because of our sins, and if they desire to establish more rigorous rules than this they have the power to do so.

Extracts from Sumptuary Laws of the Jewish Community of Metz published the 1st day of Ellul 5450 (1690) [3]

GENTLEMEN:

I have been instructed by the 9 honourable members of the Executive Commission to publish the articles of the following law which the Special Committee of 12 members has discussed and adopted. [4]

The public is warned that no one will be allowed to plead ignorance of the law as an excuse; for that reason it is published afresh drawing attention to the fact that no excuse will be accepted and that the penalties will not be waived for anyone.

Also remember gentlemen and let it be emphasized that the publication of this law is ordered in order to remove the slightest possible excuse.

No women may wear on Saturdays or festive occasions more than 4 rings. Godmothers, midwives, those who conduct the bride under the *chupah*, those who conduct her to the synagogue for the morning prayers and the young bride herself on the Saturday following her marriage are allowed to wear more than 4 rings.

Likewise the godmother, the mother on the wedding anniversary, the woman who accompanies the bride to synagogue on the morning of the wedding and she herself on the first Saturday following the wedding until leaving the synagogue; also the woman who accompanies the bride under the *chupah* from the time her *flechten* (head-dress) is put on until after the wedding ceremony.

Large or small diamonds, even imitation ones, whether solitaire or set with other stones are forbidden to everyone, men, women and young people whatever their position, even during religious ceremonies.

Gold belts, gold chains, large or small, gold coins, precious stones or pearls worn round the neck or on the arms or ears are completely forbidden. But a betrothed woman may wear any of these jewels received as a present on the first Saturday only.

Gold and silver bracelets and gold belts are expressly forbidden except to godmothers, the women who accompany the bride to the synagogue, those who accompany her there on the morning of the wedding and to midwives who are allowed to wear them up to the time they leave the synagogue. The women who accompany the bride under the *chupah* may wear them from the time she puts on her head-dress until returning from the ceremony. The young bride is allowed to wear them on the first Saturday following the wedding for the whole day.

On Saturdays and festive occasions women are allowed to wear only ordinary veils. Godmothers are allowed to wear others only on the evening before a circumcision or the Saturday following the birth of a boy. Veils of gold or silver are expressly forbidden, except on the Saturday preceding a wedding, to the mother of the bride, her mother-in-law, sisters, sisters-in-law, grandmothers and aunts. This privilege lasts for the two days before the wedding and extends to

---

[3] Original in Yiddish. Translated from the French version in *Annuaire de la Société des Etudes Juives*, Paris, 1880, i: 77 ff.
[4] The Committee of Twelve *(Commission des Douze)* was responsible for framing the laws and the Committee of Nine *(Commission des Neuf)* for enforcing them.

women who conduct the bride to the synagogue on the morning of the wedding and those who accompany her under the *chupah*.

But veils spangled with gold or pearls are permitted only to godmothers or women who accompany the bride to the synagogue on the morning of her wedding or to the bride herself on the Saturday following the wedding up to the time she leaves the synagogue. The women who accompany the bride under the *chupah* are also allowed to wear them from the moment they begin to put on the bride's head-dress until returning from the synagogue.

Midwives are allowed to wear gold or silver veils, gold belts or gold bracelets only up to the time they leave the synagogue. The same applies to the mother of a *Bar Mitzvah*.

No unmarried woman may wear a head-dress spangled with gold or with pearls except a betrothed girl on the first Saturday following the ceremony when the betrothal becomes definite and subject to a pledge. She may also do so on the two Saturdays following but only until just after the dance. On returning from the dance she must immediately take off her coiffure spangled with gold or pearls and in any case she is forbidden to go out in this attire on the Rhinport (the quay of the Moselle).

Expectant mothers and the young bride during the wedding week (who are allowed to wear all the ornaments and clothing otherwise forbidden) may not sit in front of the entrances to their houses or in the streets nor stand up or sit in front of the windows so dressed if they can be seen outside.

All coiffures made to imitate non-Jewish fashions like *godrons, en cheveux, fontanges*, are strictly forbidden but young girls under 12 years of age are allowed to wear *en cheveux* coiffures.

All ribbons of silk or taffeta of any colour except black are expressly forbidden; ribbons of silk or taffeta which women and young girls tie round their waist even black are completely forbidden but crowns and bows on these crowns are allowed whatever the material; also black ribbons worn round the neck or on the cornettes (head-dress).

Bows which women and young girls put on *juste-au-corps* or on *jaquettes* are completely forbidden whether made of ribbons of silk or taffeta and regardless of colour even black.

Manteaux plissés (pleated coats) are completely forbidden for women and young girls.

Pingwoi are forbidden for women and young girls except those under 12 years of age.

Brocades of all kinds and colours or silk material embroidered with flowers regardless of the shade are forbidden except for religious ceremonies. Nevertheless for corsages and sleeves these materials are allowed.

But the gold or silver brocades or other materials with flower patterns in gold or silver are completely forbidden to everyone even for corsages and sleeves and religious ceremonies.

All kinds of lace, braid, fringes of gold or silver or in gold or silver thread are forbidden to everyone, men, women and children, whether for clothes or for shoes or other articles of attire but this does not apply to the caps of small boys or the bonnets of women and young girls. Unmarried servant girls are not allowed to wear lace of gold or silver even imitation but they may wear on their bonnets any other kind of lace.

Shoes of red or blue leather or any other colour except black and white are forbidden to everybody. The same applies to shoes of velvet or any other material *bordées* or *piquées*.

Aprons and *moscous* may not be decorated with lace higher than a quarter of a Metz ell, including the *biais*. This applies to women married or otherwise even during fêtes and religious ceremonies.

All married women must wear top coats in the synagogue on all occasions under a penalty of one *reichsthaler*. A newly married woman is allowed in the synagogue without a top coat for the first month following her wedding.

No woman whether married or otherwise is allowed to wear two or more skirts one over the other the colours of which are different under a penalty of one *ducat*.

All wigs are forbidden to young and old alike if they are longer than those worn by priests under a penalty of one *ducat*.[5]

Buttons made of silver thread are forbidden under a penalty of one *ducat*. Those in use at the time when this law is published are permitted until the clothes are worn out.

The borders of women's coats may not exceed one quarter of a Metz ell or a little more including the lace. Moreover this type of coat is not allowed on Saturdays or festive occasions. Coats already in use which have deeper borders may be worn on ceremonial occasions and fetes.

In any case nothing spangled with gold is allowed except on ceremonial occasions under a penalty of one *ducat*.

The present law applies to everyone, men, women and children with the exception of the honourable syndics[6] and administrators, their wives, sons and unmarried daughters to whom the Articles 1, 5, 9, 10–14, 17, 24, 25, 27 and those following do not apply. But the prohibition of diamonds, gold chains, veils and borders spangled with gold or with pearls, the coiffures called *godrons* and *fontanges*, gold lace, lace wider than a quarter of a Metz ell applies to the syndics and their family as to everyone else. They are also forbidden to wear brocades, gold belts, coins, precious stones and pearls on the neck or arms.

This law also applies to all who intend to settle at Metz even for three months. They are obliged to conform from the time they arrive in the town.

It is further ordered that during week-days clothes made of velvet, silk or taffeta are forbidden regardless of colour and no matter who the person is and whether man, woman or child excepting only little velvet caps for boys and bonnets of velvet or silk for little girls which are allowed.

Any infringement of this article will be punished by a fine of one *ducat*. False sleeves and cuffs in the materials above mentioned are allowed.

No woman may walk in the streets with her collar open under a penalty of one *schilling*. Still more is it forbidden to enter the synagogue dressed in this way.

Signed: Moise, Chamass

Additional Sumptuary Laws of the Jewish Community of Metz published the 12th day of Nissan 5451 (1691)

Gentlemen:

I am instructed to publish the following in the name of the *Commission des Douze*:

Whereas a law has been made on the subject of dress and whereas new fashions are continually being introduced for women so that they are now wearing very wide trimmings with pendants and fringes and lace or braid between the trimmings and that sometimes there are even two rows of lace: therefore it is publicly announced that all these new fashions are forbidden and that the law made on the 1st Elloul 5450 must be obeyed under a penalty of one *ducat* for each offence; the same penalties still apply to veils which are too large or do not comply with the law or are decorated with lace exceeding the amount then allowed.

Marten and any other kind of fur which married women and young girls wear round their neck is equally forbidden under a penalty of one *ducat* but children may still wear it.

It has also come to the knowledge of the Council that slanderous statements are being made about the honourable members of the *Commission des Neuf* on the subject of the enforcement of these laws. The community is therefore notified that such conduct must not be repeated and that if any person continues to spread these stories he will have to pay immediately a fine of one *ducat* in addition to any other penalties ordered by the *Commission des Neuf*.

The *Commission des Neuf* wishes to draw particular attention to this regulation and will not remit any part of the penalties.

Therefore let everyone be warned and take care.

Published the 12th day of Nissan 5451 (1691) by order of the *Commission des Douze*.

Signed: Moise, Chamass

[5] During the seventeenth century Catholic priests were permitted to wear only very short wigs. [6] The *Syndics*, seven in number, formed the supreme council of the community.

Additional Sumptuary Laws of the Jewish Community of Metz published 4th Tammouz 5452 (1692)

GENTLEMEN:

I am ordered to publish the following in the names of the syndics and council of the community with whom are joined certain private members.

Whereas it has come to our knowledge that many women have their veils embroidered by non-Jews which may arouse great jealousy and animosity because formerly non-Jews were under the impression that the gold which Jewish women wore on their dress was imitation and now they know that it is real. Therefore it is announced that as from today no one, man, woman or child may directly or indirectly have veils, bonnets, coat borders or any other part of their dress embroidered by non-Jews. Any work sent out to be done by non-Jews must immediately be returned under a penalty of 20 *reichsthaler*.

I am also instructed by the *Commission des Douze* that they had considered not applying the preceding requirements to midwives, godmothers, women who conduct the bride under the *chupah*, to brides during the celebration of their marriage or the following Saturday and to mothers of a *Bar Mitzvah*. But at this moment the *Commission des Douze* has become aware of the pride, luxury and extravagance resulting from too much latitude to the extent that a large number of honourable merchants of this City are astonished at the display of luxury and wealth and their jealousy is greatly aroused against the Jews wherefore the 12 honourable members of the Commission have decided to make the following regulations:

From today and for a whole year neither midwives nor godmothers nor the others previously mentioned, may wear veils of gold or spangled with gold still less those with pearls but only plain veils with ribbons and without braid. They may not wear more than 9 rings and no diamonds. For family celebrations they may wear their Sabbath coats only and not those reserved for festivals. No belts embroidered or set with precious stones or of gold nor *sibloness* belts. No gold, no brace-lets, no chains round the neck. No clothing made of brocade whether corsage, plastron with sleeves, sleeves alone or still less any dress made entirely of this material.

No women, married or single, large or small, may wear short aprons imitating non-Jews nor scarlet coats *(manteaux ecarlates)* nor *juste-au-corps* decorated with taffeta inside or out; the same applies to dresses and coats.

In short what is forbidden to everyone in the former law made by the *Commission des Douze* is also forbidden for the period of one year to the people mentioned above for whom formerly an exception was made.

It will undoubtedly be necessary to make many further restrictions under the present circumstances but it has not been considered advisable to prohibit everything at one time.

All the offences mentioned above are subject to a penalty of one *ducat* for each offence exclusive of any other disciplinary measures which may be taken.

The Executive Commission is required to exercise an active surveillance in this matter and in no case will a fine be remitted.

This entire regulation will be inscribed in the communal register held by the *Commission des Neuf* in which the honourable members will enter the names of any offenders so that they are punished with the greatest possible severity.

Published in the synagogue by order of the council the 4th day of Tammouz 5452 (1692).

Signed: MOISE, Chamass

In 1694 the laws were revised. It was again emphasized that no fashionable coiffures were allowed. Even children were forbidden to wear ostrich feathers or fur in their hats but the council, the syndics and the physician were permitted to wear wigs of the largest size.

New regulations made in 1697 commence with a statement that the laws made in 1691 had been well received and considered fair and just. Nevertheless there was a growing tendency to neglect them and a greater trend than ever towards extravagant dress which offended Jews and non-Jews alike. Equally objectionable was the adoption of the new fashions introduced among non-Jews despite the requirement of Leviticus 18.3: 'You shall not walk in their ways'. The council therefore laid down new rules which were even stricter than those of 1691. All women except girls of fourteen or under were required to wear plain veils for synagogue and again any kind of tall coiffure worn by non-Jews was forbidden. Moreover anyone attending a ball in the town still had to conform to the dress regulations. Wigs were forbidden to young unmarried men except to hide a blemish on the head and men were not allowed to dance with their hats on.

The New Frankfurt Clothes Regulations[7]

By order of our holy community, on the instructions of the head of the community and other officials and with the consent of our excellent rabbi, whom God may keep, the following regulations were announced publicly on Thursday, 18 July 1715 in the old and new synagogues. These regulations are to be strictly observed from today for the next twenty full years.

The following regulations concerning the clothes of married and unmarried women are to be strictly observed under penalty of excommunication:

All clothes made of velvet or with gold or silver thread whether old or new, are forbidden. The same applies to *par terre* (down to the ground) clothes, with one exception. The mothers of the bride and bridegroom are allowed to wear old *par terre* clothes under the *chupah*.

From today women's clothes for Schabbes and feast-days must not be made of more than one colour. The material of which the clothes are made must not cost more than $2\frac{1}{2}$ thalers the stab. The clothes already made may be used by married and unmarried women in the following way. Clothing made of a material costing up to $3\frac{1}{2}$ florins per stab may be worn on Sabbath, even if it has more than one or two colours. Material costing from $3\frac{1}{2}$ florins up to 3 thalers per stab, may be worn only on feast-days. But clothing made of a material costing 3 thalers per stab and more is altogether forbidden in the same way as *par terre* garments.

On workdays no married or unmarried woman is allowed to wear silk clothes. Little silk caps of a single colour are allowed. Dressing gowns of silk, pleated skirts and skirts with frills are forbidden.

Married and unmarried women are forbidden to wear corselets or bodices without sleeves in the street under penalty of excommunication.

Night coats (night gowns), housecoats of silk or cotton and Leipzig caps (fur caps of marten or sable) may be worn at home, but not outside the house. Unmarried women are forbidden to wear any of these coats even in the house.

Short aprons are completely forbidden under penalty of excommunication. The same applies to curls, ringlets, false hair or powdered hair. *Fontanges* are forbidden to married and unmarried women under the same penalty.

Women, married and unmarried, are from now on forbidden to have shoes and slippers of any colour except black or with embroidery or coloured braid. But they may wear what they have got already.

Under penalty of excommunication, lace costing more than 1 florin the brabant ell (about 45 inches) is forbidden nor may it be acquired in exchange for other goods. Two kinds of lace may not be bought at the same time, nor lace together with other goods. (The reason for this prohibition is, that women might buy two kinds of lace, one cheap and one expensive or buy cheap material and expensive lace at the same time, in which case their expenditure as a whole would not exceed the permitted amount, but the lace would be of the forbidden kind.) Under the same penalty, not more than two Frankfurt ells may be used for a bonnet.

On kerchiefs and aprons no lace is allowed under the same penalty even if the garments are already made. But women are allowed to use the lace they have cut off kerchiefs and aprons, even if the lace had cost more than 1 florin for their bonnets, but not more than

---

[7] Translated from the German version in Schudt iv, Part 3, 95 ff.

2 Frankfurt ells may be used for the purpose.

Gold veils are forbidden under the same penalty. Only the mothers of the bridegroom and bride may wear them on the wedding day. But hat pins are completely forbidden under the same penalty.

Gold chains, gold belts and pendants made of precious stones are completely forbidden under the above penalty and still more so are earrings made of pearls or precious stones. Unmarried women are not allowed to wear rings of any kind.

Unmarried women should wear bonnets with black lace only. (Fine 4 thalers).

No maidservant may wear silk clothes on feast-days, Sabbaths or working days. If they transgress this law, they should be immediately removed from our community.

The head of the family and young men may not wear clothes lined with silk on workdays and less still silk clothes or silk coats on penalty of a fine of 20 thalers.

On Sabbaths and feast-days the head of the family should not wear a 'Schabbes-coat' made of silk, even if he already possesses one. Only young men, who own silk coats already may wear them. But no new silk coats may be made to measure for them or bought by them under penalty of excommunication and a fine of 20 thalers. The same applies to married men.

Coloured or white wigs are forbidden to men under penalty of excommunication.

No *Bar Mitzvah* should stand before the *Thora* wearing a wig. He should neither distribute nor send round cakes nor distribute shirts and collars. To the cantor, who has taught him, he may give a collar, but nothing else.

Heads of families and young men should not wear buttons made of spun silver or gold on their clothes. Young men should not wear on Schabbes waistcoats made of *drap d'oren* under penalty of excommunication and a fine of 10 thalers.

Nobody should wear a *tallith* made of silk on workdays (fine 2 thalers) nor may snuff be used in the synagogue. (Fine 4 thalers).

Wedding and Clothes Regulations of the Hamburg Jews 1715[8]

From now on *furbelows* (flounces: pleated borders of skirts) are forbidden on new clothes whether for married women for unmarried women or for small children. Anybody who breaks this regulation will be fined 20 thalers but whoever tries to keep it secret shall be treated as if a sacrilege had been committed.

Married and unmarried women are forbidden to wear—from top to toe—anything made of silver or gold material, anything trimmed with gold or silver, silver or gold braid or lace. They may wear hats and fur caps trimmed with gold or silver which they have already; but it is forbidden to make new hats or fur caps with gold trimmings. Lace on bonnets or breast kerchiefs is allowed.

Women are allowed hats or bonnets with one row of lace only: never a double row of lace nor high bonnets nor Berlin bonnets. The hats may not be ornamented with ribbons made into tassels or bows and no ribbon may be sewn on to the bonnet to tie it under the chin. Only a tape or cord may be used for that purpose.

Silk house-coats (*kuhr*-coats) are forbidden in two colours. Even the sashes with which they are tied must be of the same colour.

Housecoats or dressing gowns trimmed with lace or flounces are forbidden to married and unmarried women.

Velvet for dresses even for linings is forbidden to women and girls with the exception of black velvet. The bride may wear any kind of velvet under the *chupa* during her wedding. But the sashes, facings or cuffs on dresses may be made of velvet.

Bodices and neckerchiefs trimmed with lace are forbidden to women and girls, even to the bride on her wedding day; leg of mutton sleeves bordered with lace are forbidden to all women.

Diamonds, pearls or gold, even if imitation are for-

[8] Original in Yiddish. Translated from the German version in *Mittheilungen des Vereins für Hamburgische Geschichte*, Hamburg, 1903 Part 1, Nos. 3-4 (1902), 37-44.

bidden to married and unmarried women. Only a ring may be worn. But the bride may wear any type of jewellery for her engagement feast and on her wedding day.

Collars or *palatins* (a kind of stole worn over low cut dresses to hide the *décolleté*) of sable, marten or ermine are forbidden to married women and girls.

Dammel-platen are forbidden to married women but allowed to young girls on condition that they are not bordered with silver or gold.

Women and girls are allowed shoes and slippers made of black leather only without any additional ornament. Even the bridegroom must not give any other kind of footwear to his bride on her wedding day.

Polish skirts (short embroidered wide skirts), *cantouches*, boned skirts or crinolines, in short any type of skirt which is stiffened with a hoop of wire or bone or has been made stiff with other devices are forbidden to married and unmarried women. Even small children may not wear skirts of that kind.

Neckerchiefs embroidered with gold or silver are forbidden to married and unmarried women.

Married and unmarried women should not go from one place to the other, not even to Altona and not even on a working-day and definitely not to the market without top coats. They must not walk in the street or go to the synagogue on a Sabbath or feast-day without top coats; they are allowed however to walk as far as three doors away from their home without it, but not further.

Beauty-plasters on the face are forbidden to married women and girls, but they may be worn in the *dünne* (inside the arm).

Palatins (stoles which were often made of transparent material) are forbidden to married and unmarried women with one exception, that is, if they are made of black velvet without tassels or silk fringes and definitely without silver or gold which must not be embroidered on the material or added to it in the form of a braid or border.

Gold and silver ribbons on *fontanges* and *flegen* are forbidden even to young girls.

It is forbidden for unmarried men and women to learn to dance. (Fine 20 thalers). Whoever breaks this law openly or in secret will be excommunicated as if he had committed a sacrilege.

No three women, married or unmarried and still less more than that number, should take a walk in the evening without rainwear; on Sabbath or feast-day no women, married or unmarried should sit in big groups in front of the door.

Hats ornamented with tassels or feathers, hats made of gold material even without tassels and lastly hats trimmed with silver or gold braid or lace are forbidden to girls and small children.

Women or girls who wear silk house coats of one colour, or simple dressing gowns in the house or put on wraps of gold material, or fur capes trimmed with gold or silver which they have acquired earlier (before the regulations) should under no circumstances go out in the street in them without top coats and without special covers for their caps. It is forbidden too to sit in any of these clothes in front of the door.

Topcoats with lace or braid are forbidden to married and unmarried women. New clothes of silk are also forbidden. It is forbidden to introduce any new fashion whatever it may be.

The godmother should bring the child to the synagogue with only two other women and they should wear topcoats even on a working day. They should not go to the synagogue in carriages except when it is raining very hard. They should not give any presents with the exception of swaddling clothes which must not be trimmed with silver or gold, because that has been forbidden since olden times.

No maid servant should wear gold or silver lace on her cap, nor shawls of silver or gold threaded material *(drap d'or)* nor bows or head-dress made of ribbons. She should not wear silk dresses and should not have any new embroidered skirts made for her. (Fine one thaler.)

Wives and children of doctors are also subject to the laws and regulations cited above.

Silver and gold trimmings on coats and waistcoats, buttons made of silver and gold wire, gold materials *(drap d'or)* and velvet even for linings are forbidden to married and unmarried men. Only waistcoats of black velvet are allowed.

In all cases of death in the family which may God prevent women are not allowed to follow the coffin without a topcoat.

It is not permitted to travel in a carriage to a wedding. Only the bride and three bridesmaids may do so; all other guests are only allowed to use one if it is raining hard. Neither married nor unmarried women should go to a wedding without topcoats. This applies both ways to and from the synagogue. Neither the coachman nor the horses of the bridal carriage should be adorned with ribbons.

Anyone who breaks one of the above laws in which no fine is mentioned should pay the first time two thalers the second time 4 thalers. But if the law concerning diamonds, pearls and gold is broken the offender should pay the first time 4 thalers, the second time double the amount and the third time it will be left to the discretion of the people who administer the law to punish the offender according to their own judgement.

From to-day until further notice no silk dresses of two colours should be made for women with the exception of dark grey and brown. (Fine 20 thalers.) Whoever offends openly or in secret will be excommunicated and treated as somebody who has sinned against God.

Moreover, nobody is allowed to make a crown or wreath for the bridegroom (not even as a present) to put on top of his *tallith* with which he covers his head. The *tallith* may be made only of white mohair with a four finger wide golden braid at the borders. The cap too must be made of silver white mohair and trimmed with a narrow silver braid or lace. In case the bride's dowry however amounts to 5000 thalers or more the bridegroom is allowed to wear whatever he pleases.

Whoever gives to his daughter 400 Thaler or less for a dowry may not give her silk dresses. But if the parents of a girl who is betrothed have bought such clothes already they have to declare in public on their conscience that they have bought these things before the regulations came into force. Otherwise they will

be fined 10 thalers.

The presents from the bridegroom to the bride should be of the following value from now on. If the dowry is under 5000 thalers the bridegroom may not give any presents worth more than 5% of the dowry. The bride may not give anything worth more than 2% of this amount. If the dowry amounts to 5000 thalers or more the bridegroom may give as much as he likes. Whoever breaks this law will be fined 100 thalers. But whoever employs cunning or trickery in these matters will be excommunicated as if he had sinned against God.

Given in the year 1715

Sumptuary Laws of Carpentras, 26 Heshvan 5499 (9 November 1738) [9]

We, the undersigned, observing the envy of people, how everyone strives to outdo his friend, so that rich and poor cannot be distinguished and all want to look important and wealthy, both in their clothes and their jewellery, and women who cannot afford it, borrow money from Gentiles and become impoverished . . . we have fasted for three days to mend our ways . . . On Saturday night, Parashat Leikh Lekha, on the 12th day of the month of Marcheshvan, there were gathered the elders and members of the community, and others, apart from Moshe Drukomoartino, who is ill, and Jacob Nakit, who was not in the synagogue because of his age, and it was decided to appoint seven representatives of the community who decreed the following changes against which there will be no appeal.

No man, whether married or single, may wear a wig which is not completely round and it may not have a ribbon, curl, a bag enclosing the tail or powder. But the first powder, which is needed for combing it is allowed. Also, no man, whether married or single is allowed to wear any garment apart from an *elbuf* and over it a *carcassonne*. For summer clothes, they are allowed to wear only a *camelot de boursal*, an *estamina*,

[9] Translated from the Hebrew in C. Roth, *Sumptuary Laws of the Community of Carpentras*, in *Jewish Quarterly Review* 1928 xviii: No. 4.

an *estimina de bougin* and a *camelot* of hair over it and no other *samura* of wool and silk. No garments of silk or lined with silk are allowed and above all, no silver nor gold, whether on the buttons or the buttonholes. Those who already have garments which we have forbidden, will be allowed to wear them as long as they last, but they may not have on them gold or silver and the silk cuff or facing must be removed. Garments made of silk or lined with silk may be worn as long as they last.

A man, whether married or single, may buy second-hand garments of the kind forbidden provided there is neither gold nor silver on them.

No short decorative waistcoat may be made called *coureuse* and no waistcoat for girls called *basin de flandres*, whether short or long. *Justaucorps* may not be lined with muslin and the short waistcoats called *curosoa* may be worn provided the silk facing is taken off.

No man, married or single, may wear decorated cuffs on his garments or on his hands made of any kind of lace. Also, he is not allowed to wear a ring on his fingers, except a round golden one and if it has a stone it may not be a diamond or a stone of great value. Also it is forbidden to buy any new Stockings of silk and shoes called *escarpins* (i.e. without heels) but those who have them already may wear them as long as they last. On no account may a silver buckle be worn on shoes or on garters but a silver button on cuffs is allowed. If a man is able to buy old silk stockings he may wear them.

No woman, whether married or single, is allowed to wear a garment of velvet with silk braid with a floral design or multi-coloured, whether new or old, and also no garment made of silk with flower designs in various colours. The *agagnau* (a divided mantle) and the *camisole* may be made of damask, of silk or any other material apart from velvet with flower designs without any silver or gold on them. Those who have cuffs or facings of silver or gold without plaits or lace may wear them but from now on may not pay more than one *écu* and three francs for each piece, and those who have laced bodices of velvet with silk braid or of a silk material with silver and gold flowers, may wear them provided there are no plaits or silver or gold lace on them and they must not be made of damask. Those bodices that are still permitted may not be worn without one camisole or robe. Unmarried girls who wear a band in their hair, whether of gold or silver may continue to wear one so long as it lasts but they may not buy any more bands of silver or gold. On no account are silk slippers allowed but those who have them already may wear them provided they take off the silver and gold.

No woman, whether married or single, is allowed more than two lace scarves nor may they make new ones until they are worn out, unless they wish to use them as a coif, in which case they may make two others. And those who already have more than two, may only use two until they are worn out, or unless they make a coif as mentioned above. But they may have as many other scarves with borders as they desire also two aprons with lace. They are also allowed to make *cubertas* and handkerchiefs with lace as they choose.

Unmarried girls are not allowed to wear a coif called *jouinessa* with a ribbon attached nor a ribbon in front of the bodice called *escala*.

A man's wife and daughters may not between them wear ornaments of silver or gold, diamond or other precious stones, on their neck, or on their arms or fingers exceeding 20 *écus* in value or pearls exceeding 100 *écus* in value.

They are allowed to wear a belt of silver and a *cornet* and three rings with not more than one diamond apart from the wedding ring which is called *signet* which is not included in the three. A gold clasp is allowed round the neck as well as golden earrings and a velvet collar. Boys and girls up to five years may wear all kinds of lace but garments with silver and gold on them are allowed only until they are worn out.

Bibliography

ABRAHAMS, I. *Jewish Life in the Middle Ages*, London, 1932

ABRAHAMS, Israel & COOK, S.A. in *Encyclopaedia Biblica*, 1899. s.v. Dress, Fringes, Mitre, Shoes, Tunic, Turban

ADDISON, L. *The Present State of the Jews*, London, 1675

ADLER, E.N. *Jews in Many Lands*, London, 1905

AMIRA, K. von, *Die Dresdener Bilderhandschrift des Sachsenspiegels,* facsimile. Leipzig, 1902

AMIRA, K. von, *Die Dresdener Bilderhandschrift des Sachsenspiegels,* II: *Erläuterungen,* Part I. Leipzig, 1925

ARONIUS, J. *Regesten zur Geschichte der Juden in Fränkischen und Deutschen Reiche bis zum jahr 1273,* Berlin 1887–1902

BACHER, W. *Un Episode de l'histoire des Juifs de Perse* in *Revue des Etudes Juives* XLVII

BARNETT, R.D. *Four Sculptures from Amman* in *Annual of the Department of Antiquities of Jordan,* I, 1951

BARON, S.W. *A Social and Religious History of the Jews.* Vol. III. New York, 1957

BARTLETT, W.H. *Walks about Jerusalem,* London, 1844

BAUER, J. *Le Chapeau Jaune Chez les Juifs Comtadins* in *Revue des Etudes Juives* XXXVI

BEAUCLERK, G. *Journey to Morocco,* London, 1828

BECK, J.J. *Tractatus de Juribus Judaeorum,* Nuremberg, 1731

BENJAMIN, J.J. *Eight Years in Asia and Africa from 1846 to 1855,* Hanover, 1863

BEN-ZVI, I. *The Exiled and The Redeemed,* Philadelphia, 1957

BERLINER, A. *Aus Dem Leben Der Deutschen Juden im Mittelalter,* Berlin, 1900

BERTMAN, S. *Tasseled Garments in the Ancient East Mediterranean* in *The Bible Archaeologist,* Dec. 1961. Vol. XXIV, No. 4

BESANCENET, J. *Costumes du Maroc,* Paris, 1942

BOECKLER, A. *Die frühmittelalterlichen Bronzetüren.* Vol. III: *Die Bronzetür von Verona.* Marburg a.L., 1931

BOEHN, M. von, *Die Mode. Menschen und Moden im Mittelalter . . . .* Munich, 1925

BOENER, J.A. *Kurze Bericht von dem Alterthum und Freyheiten des freyen Hof-Markts Furth,* 1705

BOTTA, M.P.E. *Monument de Ninive,* Paris, 1849

BRATTON, F.G. *A History of the Bible,* London, 1961

BRITISH MUSEUM. *Catalogue of the Ivory Carvings of the Christian Era,* London, 1919

BRITISH MUSEUM. *Guide to the early Christian and Byzantine Antiquities,* London, 1921

BRÜLL, A. *Trachten der Juden im Nachblischen Alterthume*, Frankfurt A/M, 1873

BRUYN, C. de, *Reizen*, Delft, 1698

BUDGE, E. A. W. *Amulets and Superstitions*, London, 1930

BURNES, A. *Travels in Bokhara in 1830*, London, 1837

CAHEN, A. *Règlements Somptuaires de la Communauté Juive de Metz a la Fin Du XVIIe Siècle* in *Annuaire de la Société des Etudes Juives* I, 1881

CHAPPELLE, G. de La, *Recueil de divers Portraits* (Paris, 1650?)

CHARLES-ROUX, J. *Le Costume en Provence*, Paris, 1907

CHISHULL, E. *Travels in Turkey and back to England*, London, 1747

CINTAS, P. *Amulettes Puniques*, 1946, *Pubs. de l'Institut Des Hautes Etudes de Tunis*

CORSON, R. *Fashions in Hair*, London, 1965

CORYAT, T. *Coryat's Crudities*, Glasgow, 1905

CUNNINGTON, C. W. & P. *Handbook of English Mediaeval Costume*, London, 1952. *Handbook of English Costume in the Eighteenth Century*, London, 1957. *A Dictionary of English Costume*, London, 1960

CURZON, G. N. *Persia and the Persian Question*, London, 1892

DANDINI, J. *A Voyage to Mount Libanus*, London, 1811

DANON, A. *La Communauté Juive de Salonique Au XVIe Siècle* in *Revue des Etudes Juives* XL

DAVENPORT, M. *The Book of Costume*, New York, 1948

DEMIDOV, A. N. *Voyage dans la Russie Méridionale et la Crimée . . . Executé en 1837*, Paris, 1840. (Album of Plates . . . drawn and lithographed by Raffet, Paris, 1848)

DODWELL, C. R. *The Great Lambeth Bible*, London, 1959

DUBNOW, S. M. *History of the Jews in Russia and Poland*, Philadelphia, 1916

DUMAS, A. *Tangier to Tunis*, Trans. and ed. A. E. Murch, London, 1959

EHRENSTEIN, T. *Das Alte Testament im Bilde*, Vienna, 1923

ELJASZ, W. *Ubiory w Polsce*, Cracow, 1879 (on mediaeval Polish costume)

Encyclopaedia Biblica, London, 1899

Encyclopaedia of Islam, s.v. Kalansuwa

Encyclopaedia Judaica, Berlin, 1928–34

EVANS, J. *Dress in Mediaeval France*, London, 1952

EWALD, P. *Reise . . . Von Tunis Nach Tripolis*, Nuremberg, 1842

FAKHRY, Ahmed, *The Necropolis of El-Bagwat in Kharga Oasis*, Cairo, 1951

FERRIOL, M. de, *Recueil de cent estampes* . . . Paris, 1714

FINKELSTEIN, L. *Jewish Self-Government in the Middle Ages*, New York, 1964

FINN, E. A. *Home in the Holy Land*, London, 1866

FINN, J. *The Jews in China*, London, 1843

FLÜGEL, J. C. *The Psychology of Clothes*, London, 1930

FOX-DAVIES, A. C. *A Complete Guide to Heraldry*, London, 1925

FRIEDBERG, C. B. *Bet Eked Sepharim*, 2nd ed. Tel-Aviv, 1952. (Bibliography of Hebrew books.)

GARNETT, L. M. J. *The Women of Turkey*, London, 1891

GARRUCCI, P. R. *Storia della Arte Cristiana*, Prato, 1873–81

GASTER, M. *Samaritan Phylacteries and Amulets*, in *Studies and Texts*, London, 1925–28

GASTER, M. *The Samaritans*, London, 1925

GASTER, T. H. *The Holy and the Profane*, New York, 1955

GEBHARDT, O. von. *The Miniatures of the Ashburnham Pentateuch*, London, 1883

GILYAROVSKAYA, N. *Russkii Istorich Kostyum*, Moscow, 1945

GODBEY, A. H. *The Lost Tribes A Myth*, Durham, N. C., 1930. Chap. XIII 'Persian, Turkoman, Mongol and Chinese Jews.'

GOETZ, H. *The History of Persian Costume*, in Pope III

GOLD, H. *Die Juden und Judengemeinden Mährens*, Brünn, 1929

GOLDSCHMIDT, A. *Die Elfenbeinskulpturen aus der zeit der Karolingischen und Sächsischen Kaiser VIII–XI jahrhundert*, Berlin, 1914

GOLDSTEIN, M. & DRESDNER, K. *Kultura i sztuka ludu zydowskiego na ziemiach polskich*, Lwow, 1935 (The Culture and Art of the Jewish People in Poland)

GOODENOUGH, E. R. *Jewish Symbols in the Graeco-Roman Period*, Vols. I–XI, New York, 1953–64

GORDON, C. H. *Before The Bible*, London, 1962

GOULVEN, J. *Les Mellahs de Rabat-Salé*, Paris, 1927

GRAETZ, H. *History of the Jews*, London, 1901

GRAYZEL, S. *The Church and the Jews in the XIIIth century*, Philadelphia, 1933

GRUNWALD, M. *Trachten der Juden in Jüdisches Lexikon* V (Eng. translation in *Universal Jewish Encyc.* III *s.v. Costumes*)

GURNEY, O. R. *The Hittites*, London, 1961

HAEDO, Diego de, *Topographia E Historia General de Argel*, Valladolid, 1612

HAHN, Joseph Nordlingen, *Sefer Yosef Ometz*, Frankfurt A/M, 1723 (new ed. 1928), Secs. 3 and 592 on the *Sarbal*

HAMDY-BEY & LAUNAY, M. de, *Les Costumes Populaires de La Turquie en 1873*, Constantinople, 1873

HAMERTON, J. A., Ed. *Peoples of All Nations*, London, 1922–24

HARFF, Arnold von, *The Pilgrimage of* . . . translated from the German, London, Hakluyt Society, 1946

HARGREAVES-MAWDSLEY, W. N. *A History of Academical Dress in Europe*, Oxford, 1963

HARGREAVES-MAWDSLEY, W. N. *A History of Legal Dress in Europe*, Oxford, 1963

HARRISON, M. *The History of the Hat*, London, 1960

HEATON, E. W. *Everyday Life in Old Testament Times*, London, 1956

HENDERSON, E. *Biblical Researches and Travels in Russia including a Tour in the Crimea . . . with observations on the state of the Rabbinical and Karaite Jews . . .* London, 1826

HENTZE, C. *Chinese Tomb Figures*, London, 1928

HESSE-WARTEG, de, *Tunis, the Land and the People*, London, 1882

HEUZEY, L. & J. *Histoire du Costume dans l'Antiquité Classique—L'Orient*, Paris, 1935

HILER, H. *From Nudity to Raiment*, London, 1929

HOBSON, R. L., *Art of the Chinese Potter*, London, 1923

HOBSON, R. L. *The George Eumorfopoulous Collection Catalogue*, London, 1925

HOLLAENDERSKI, L. *Les Israélites de Pologne*, Paris, 1846

HÖLSCHER, U. *The Excavation of Medinet Habu—Vol. IV. The Mortuary Temple of Ramses III* Part 2, Chicago, 1951

HÖST, G. *Nachrichten von Marokos und Fes*, Copenhagen, 1781

HOTTENROTH, F. *Le Costume . . . des peuples anciens et modernes*, Paris, 1883–92

HOTTENROTH, F. *Handbuch der Deutschen Tracht*, Stuttgart, 1895–96

HOTTENROTH, F. *Deutsche Volkstrachten*, Frankfurt Am Main, 1898

HOTTENROTH, F. *Altfrankfurter Trachten*, Frankfurt Am Main, 1912

HOUSTON, M. G. *Ancient Egyptian Mesopotamian and Persian Costume*, London, 1954. *Mediaeval costume in England and France*, London, 1939

HUGHES, P. *The Church In Crisis. A History of the Twenty Great Councils*, London, 1961

HYAMSON, A. M. *The Sephardim of England*, London, 1951

International Standard Bible Encyclopaedia, Chicago, 1930. *s.v.* Dress

The Interpreter's Bible, New York, 1952

JASTROW, M. *A Dictionary of the Targum, the Talmud Babli and Yerushalmi*, New York, 1950

The Jewish Encyclopaedia, New York, 1902

JOHNSON, R. *Travels through part of the Russian Empire and the country of Poland along the southern shores of the Baltic*, London, 1815

JOSEPHUS, *Loeb Classical Library* ed. 1926

JOUIN, J. *Le Costume de la Femme Israélite au Maroc* in *Journal de la Société des Africanistes*, Paris, 1936

Jüdisches Lexikon, Berlin, 1930

KENDRICK, A. F. *Victoria and Albert Museum. Catalogue of Textiles from Burying-Grounds in Egypt.* Vol. I. Graeco-Roman Period. London, 1920

KISCH, B. *History of the Jewish Pharmacy (Judenapothek) in Prague* in *Historia Judaica* VIII, New York, 1946

KISCH, G. *The Jews in Medieval Germany*, Chicago, 1949

KISCH, G. *The Yellow Badge in History* in *Historia Judaica* XIX No. 2. New York, 1957

KRAELING, E. G. *The Synagogue. The Excavations at Dura-Europos*, New Haven, 1956

KRAUSS, S. *Griechische und Lateinische Lehnwörter im Talmud, Midrasch und Targum*, Berlin, 1899

KRAUSS, S. *Kleidung im Mittelalter* in *Encyc. Judaica* X

KRETSCHMER, A. & ROHRBACH, C. *Die Trachten der Volker*, Leipzig, 1860–4

LANE, E. W. *Manners and Customs of the Modern Egyptians* Everyman ed. London, 1954

LAWSON, C. A. *British and Native Cochin*, Cochin, 1860

LELOIR, M. *Dictionnaire du Costume*, Paris, 1951

LEMPRIERE, W. *A Tour through the Dominions of the Emperor of Morocco*, Newport, 1813

LENZ, O. *Timbuktu. Reise Durch Marokko, Die Sahara Und Den Sudan . . . in Den Jahren 1879 Und 1880*, Leipzig, 1892

LETTS, M. *The Sachsenspiegel and its Illustrators*, London, 1933

LEVY, Moritz, *Die Sephardim in Bosnien*, Sarajevo, 1911

LEVY, R. *A Baghdad Chronicle*, Cambridge, 1929

LEVY, R. *Notes on Costume from Arabic Sources* in *Journal of the Royal Asiatic Society*, London, 1935, pp. 319–38

LICHTENSTADTER, I. *The Distinctive Dress of Non-Muslims in Islamic Countries* in *Historia Judaica*, New York, 1943, V, No. 1

LILIEN, E. M. *List of the original etchings*, Berlin-Vienna, 1922

LINDO, E.H. *The History of the Jews of Spain and Portugal*, London, 1848

LORD, P.B. *Algiers with Notices of the Neighbouring States of Barbary*, London, 1835

LOVILLO, J. Guerrero, *Las Cantigas*, Madrid, 1949

LUTZ, H.F. *Textiles and Costumes among the Peoples of the Ancient Near East*, Leipzig, 1923

LYON, G.F. *A Narrative of Travels in North Africa*, London, 1821

MACDONALD, J. *Palestinian Dress* in *Palestine Exploration Quarterly*, London, Jan.-April, 1951

MACMICHAEL, W. *Journey from Moscow to Constantinople*, London, 1819

MAHLER, J.G. *The Westerners Among The Figurines of the T'Ang Dynasty of China*, Rome, 1959

MARCAIS, G. *Le Costume Musulman D'Alger*, Paris, 1930

MARCUS, J.R. *The Jew in the Mediaeval World*, Cincinnati, 1938

MAYER, L.A. *Mamluk Costume*, Geneva, 1952

MAYER, N. *The Jews of Turkey*, London, 1913

MENDELSSOHN, S. *The Jews of Africa*, London, 1920

MILANO, A. *Storia degli ebrei in Italia*, Turin, 1963

MINORSKY, V. *The Chester Beatty Library. A Catalogue of the Turkish Manuscripts and Miniatures*, Dublin, 1958

Monumenta Judaica, Cologne, 1963

MOREY, C.F. *Early Christian Art*, Princeton New Jersey, 1953

MULLER, D.H. & SCHLOSSER, J.v. *Die Haggadah von Sarajevo*, Vienna, 1898

New Schaff-Herzog Encyclopaedia of Religious Knowledge, New York, 1909, *s.v.* Dress

NICOLAY, N. de, *Les Quatre Premiers Livres des Navigations . . . Orientales*, Lyons, 1568

NORBLIN, J.P. *Collection de Costumes Polonais*, Paris, 1817

NORRIS, H. *Costume and Fashion*, London, 1924

NORRIS, H. *Church Vestments*, London, 1949

OPPENHEIM, M. *Bilder aus dem Altjüdischen Familienleben*, Frankfurt A/M, 1886 (Drawings dated 1866–69)

PAHLEN, K.K. *Mission to Turkestan*, ed. R.A. Pierce, London, 1964

PARKES, J. *The Conflict of the Church and the Synagogue*, Philadelphia, 1961

PARROT, A. *Nineveh and the Old Testament*, London, 1955

PARROT, A. *Samaria. The Capital of the Kingdom of Israel*, London, 1958

PFISTER, R. *Les Débuts du Vêtement Copte* in *Etudes D'Orientalisme* . . . Le Musée Guimet II, Paris, 1932

PFISTER, R. *Textiles de Palmyre*, Paris, 1934

PFISTER, R. & BELLINGER, L. *The Excavations at Dura-Europos*. Final Report IV. Part II. The Textiles. New Haven, 1945

PICART, B. *Ceremonies et Coutumes Religieuses de tous les Peuples du Monde*, Amsterdam, 1723–43. First English edition, 1731

PICKEN, M. B. *The Fashion Dictionary*, New York, 1957

PLANCHÉ, J. R. *A Cyclopaedia of Costume*, London, 1876

POCKNEE, C. E. *Liturgical Vesture*, London, 1960

POPE, A. U. *A Survey of Persian Art*, London and New York, 1938–9

PRILUTSKY, N. *Dos Gevet*, Warsaw, 1923

PRITCHARD, J. B. *The Ancient Near East in Pictures*, Princeton, New Jersey, 1954

PRODAN, M. *The Art of the Tang Potter*, London, 1960

PURCHAS, S. *Purchas His Pilgrimes*, Glasgow, 1905

RACINET, M. A. *Le Costume Historique*, Paris, 1888

RÉAU, L. *Iconographie de l'Art Chrétien*, II, Paris, 1956

RICHARDSON, H. G. *The English Jewry under Angevin Kings*, London, 1960

RICE, D. Talbot, *The Beginnings of Christian Art*, London, 1957

RICE, D. Talbot, *Art of the Byzantine Era*, London, 1963

RICHTER, J. P. & TAYLOR, A. C. *The Golden Age of Classic Christian Art*, London, 1904

ROBERT, Ulysse, *Les Signes D'Infamie Au Moyen Age*, Paris, 1891

ROGER, E. *La Terre Sainte*, Paris, 1664

ROSENZWEIG, A. *Kleidung Und Schmuck Im Biblischen Und Talmudischen Schriftum*, Berlin, 1905

ROTH, C. *The History of the Jews of Italy*, Philadelphia, 1946

RUBENS, A. (i) *Anglo-Jewish Portraits*, London, 1935; (ii) *A Jewish Iconography*, London, 1954

RÜNSBERG, E. von, *Der Sachsenspiegel. Bilder aus der Heidelberger Handschrift*, Leipzig, 1934

SALAMÉ, A. *A Narrative of the Expedition to Algiers in the Year 1816*, London, 1819

SANDYS, G. *Sandys Travailes*, 5th Ed. London, 1652

SASSOON, D. S. *A History of the Jews in Baghdad*, Letchworth, 1949

SCHEMEL, S. *Die Kleidung der Juden im Zeitalter der Mischnah*, Berlin, 1912

SCHIPPER, I. *Kultur Geschichte*, Warsaw, 1926

SCHUDT, J. K. *Jüdische Merkwürdigkeiten*, Frankfurt and Leipzig, 1714–18

SEGAL, J. B. *The Hebrew Passover. From the earliest time to A.D. 70*, London, 1963

SEYRIG, H. *Armes et Costumes Iraniens de Palmyre* in *Syria* XVIII, Paris, 1937

SIBMACHER, J. *Wappenbuch*, Nuremberg, 1856–1936

SKIPPON, P. *An Account of a Journey*, London, 1746

STERN, S. *The Court Jew*, Philadelphia, 1950

STRAUS, R. *The Jewish Hat as an aspect of Social History* in *Jewish Social Studies* IV, New York, 1942

STRAUSS, E. *The Social Isolation of Ahl Adh-Dhimma* in *Etudes Orientales à la Mémoire de Paul Hirschler*, Budapest, 1950

SUKENIK, E. L. *The Ancient Synagogue of Beth Alpha*, Jerusalem, 1932

TCHERIKOVER, V. *Hellenistic Civilization and the Jews*, Philadelphia, 1961

THEVENOT, M. de, *Voyages*, Amsterdam, 1727

TOBAR, J. *Les Inscriptions Juives de K'ai-Fong-Fou*, Shanghai, 1900

TRISTRAM, E. W. *English Mediaeval Wall Painting . . . The 13th century*, Oxford, 1950

TRITTON, A. S. *Islam and the Protected Religions* in *Journal of the Royal Asiatic Society*, London, 1927

ULRICHS, J. C. *Sammlung Jüdischer Geschichten . . . in der Schweiz*. Basel, 1768

The Universal Jewish Encyclopaedia, New York, 1948

VAN LENNEP, H. J. *The Oriental Album*, New York, 1862

VAUX, R. de, *Ancient Israel*, London, 1961

VINAVER, S. *Spomenica*, Belgrade, 1924

WELLESZ, E. *The Vienna Genesis*, London, 1960

WHITE, W. C. *Chinese Jews*, Toronto, 1942

WILPERT, J. *Die Römischen Mosaiken und Malereien der Kirchlichen Bauten vom IV bis XIII Jahrhundert*, Frieburg im Breisgau, 1917

WILSON, J. *The Lands of the Bible*, Edinburgh, 1847

WISCHNITZER-BERNSTEIN, R. *Symbole und Gestalten der Jüdischen Kunst*, Berlin, 1935

WOOLLEY, C. L. *Ur of the Chaldees*, London, 1929

WOOLLEY, C. L. *Mesopotamia and the Middle East*, London, 1961

Glossarial Index